My Dad's Thoughts
Bits and Pieces of Life

By

Ruben Dozal, Jr.

RoseDog Books

PITTSBURGH, PENNSYLVANIA 15222

ISBN # 0-8059-9859-4
Printed in the United States of America

First Printing

For information or to order additional books, please write:
RoseDog Books
701 Smithfield St.
Pittsburgh, PA 15222
U.S.A.
1-800-834-1803
Or visit our web site and
on-line bookstore at www.rosedogbookstore.com

Dedication

To Page Jones-Goulding tutor from The Vision Literacy Program.
You are not only my tutor but my friend. Thank you for all your help
and support.

Table of Contents

A Good Teacher

Judge me not for the clothes I wear, nor the way I speak or look, but by the work I do, which is always to the best of my ability.

If I am wrong in some task do not be afraid to tell me so, but if I do right pat yourself on the back because you have taught me well.

The hardest thing to do is to please the man in charge or the teacher.

And in some cases yourself.

We all try hard to do a good job but without some kind of leadership our good deeds could be the wrong ones.

That's why I say again, if the work is done right the first time, pat yourself on the back for you have taught me well.

© Ruben Dozal Jr. 4/12/98

Words of The Heart

Since the bottle of my imprisonment was opened, I lost the fear of words and the pen of heat entered my frozen fingers. I cannot stop writing.

When the door of knowledge was revealed unto my eyes and opened it I did, my loife has been change for the good. I love to say I can read better also I can write without fear of spelling words wrong because I can correct them later.

I have been in a bottle looking out, year after year until I was almost fifty years old and I still could not read or write very well at all.

The closing of my education stopped almost thirty–five years earlier, I lie to you not.

My story is not great, it is not new, but it is my story and I kept everything in my mind and soul until now.

I am not proud of my education but I am proud about what I have done without it.

I do not stand alone in the darkness of ignorance for I had the power to turn on the light, to make my life reach the roads of life.

I do not know the force that keeps pushing me for my thoughts are all within me and the words just keep on coming out non-stoppable onto the paper of fire.

© Ruben Dozal Jr. 10/13/2004

Beautiful Ride

Do not cry for me for my journey is about to end and it has been a ride of all rides not knowing what was at the next curve or hill. The expectations were surpassed by the surprises, which were shocking, but also received with open arms.

I have enjoyed my life to its fullest. So go forth embracing the light of good which is all around you.

Be happy, for only you can find happiness. Do not look for it in other people but within you own soul.

Remember this day and also what I have done. To others it is nothing, but to my loved ones maybe a thought or two in the years to come.

So go and enjoy life for today.

© 1/9/99 by Ruben Dozal Jr.

Big Bear

Every time I go over to see you, it seems like my heart just breaks into pieces.

I know that you can see me; I also know that you do not know who I am. Every time I pick you up in my arms and you cry out in pain, I also cry in pain.

When I move you around a little and try to help you move your arms and legs and you cry out the painful cries, you yell out, I feel it right to the deepest part of my broken heart.

Out of all the sons-in-law that you have, I am considered the meanest and toughest one to talk to. Because of my character, which at times is very intimidating, sometimes it is hard for me not to take a step back.

But all in all I am The Big Bear who loves all of you the most and tries to help in my own quiet way.

I cannot tell you all these things that you could understand, because your Alzheimer's has stolen everything from your mind except the light of day.

Your son-in-law, Ruben.

© By Ruben Dozal Jr. 5/10/99

Bitter Taste

I am big and I am strong.

I am bitter and I am sweet.

But sometimes I am small and mean.

I can make you a new person.

I can make you a happy person.

I can make you a sad person and this you know, but you cannot leave me for I am in your soul and taking over your mind also.

Thinking that I am good for you, not giving in until you have lost it all.

Still thinking that you are in control, still thinking that you do not have a problem which you do not, for I am the victor in this soul.

And move aside, here comes the next one to taste my bitter taste.

By Ruben Dozal Jr. 8/9/99

BOY TO MAN

"It is time," a poor and weary woman tells her husband. So the husband, after working fifteen hours that day, gets up at two in the morning to take his loving wife to the hospital, so she can have her firstborn. In the excitement the husband hopes that his car will start okay and it did. At the hospital they tell him to wait outside, so he does, nervous and thinking all the time, *I hope everything comes all right.* Moments later he is given the good news- - you have a son! He cries but he is not sure if it is out of happiness or sadness for he is a poor man in wealth but rich in the love for his wife and new son.

"Come, my husband, hold my hand and see your son." With tears in his eyes he tells his wife, "I hope to God that I will be a good father."

"Why do you cry my husband?"

"Because I know that my seed will continue and my God will help me see my son become a man in his own time."

And with that, time went on and the boy who was five asked his mother how come his father never had time to talk to him or play with him. His mother tried to explain, but could not. So twelve years goes by, the son comes home with tattoos on his body and wearing a colors bandana. The mother does not know what it means nor does the father because of work, always working long hard hours. And when he comes home late at night all the father wants to do is have dinner, take a shower and go to bed. But on this night it was different because he saw his son all grown up, and the direction that his only son was heading brought silent tears to his eyes and broken heart.

Because in his heart was the feeling of failure in not keeping his word at the hospital when his boy was born. Now almost a man, that was more than he could endue. So in the following week he started making arrangements that would allow him to spend more time with his son. And on that Friday he was given the okay to just work eight hours on every Friday.

Feeling good and happy about this, the father hurries home for a chance to talk to his son. Just three blocks away from home he sees some kids in a fight, but he was too far away to see who it was. So he got closer and in terror sees his son being beaten by four gang members. He stops the car, jumps out to help his son, and sees one of them pull out a gun. Four shots were fired hitting the father who jumped in the way so that his son might live. When the boy turned around to see his father who had taken the four shots for him, it completely shocked him for he knew that he was bringing shame to his father by not respecting his name.

Later at the hospital the doctor asked, "Who can identify this man?"
The boy answered, "I can, he is my father."
The boy waited and waited for five days to hear the news about his father. Then the doctor came and talked to him, "You can go see him now." The boy got up and ran to the room where his father is. Seeing his father in a state of near death, he asked, "Why dad, why"?

The dad opens his eyes with tears coming down slowly and answers, "You are my only son and I love you, my son." With those words the young man was shocked because he thought his father did not care about him.

Now the young man was caught with a choice, to choose between good and evil.

Two weeks passed and the young man returned to his old ways. He came to the meeting place of his fellow members and being the leader and the best fighter, not much was said until one of the new members joking around asked, "Hey, did you hear about that old man taking four slugs for his kid"? Then total silence.

All the old members looked to the leader for a response.

"Yes, I did. He was my Father."

The young man then picks up his hands, puts them behind his head, undoes his bandana and drops it to the floor. Then he takes his jacket off and drops it to the floor too, and Walks Out A Man.

The man goes home and changes his clothes, to his mother's surprise.

When she sees him, she could not believe her eyes; her son had turned into a man. No words were said, just a happy look on his mother's face, that's all.

When the father sees his son the way he is, again, nothing was said —just tears coming from his Father's eyes out of happiness.

In very soft words, the Father tells his son, "Thank you, my son."

The boy has become a man before his loving Father's Eyes.
© by Ruben Dozal Jr. 12/15/98

My dear and beloved brother

Why do you not see your hands in front of you,
are they not the same?

So is the love of the rest of our family –
do not ease them out.
They hunger and feel just like you.
They also feel the pain of your sons,
which at this moment is tearing you apart inside.

Fear not for them at this moment for
the hand of the Lord is with you and them.
You have given love and kindness to them.
You have taught them right from wrong and the
difference between good and evil.
The rest is up to them to decide.
They must choose and experience
the fruits of their choosing alone.

Look beyond the final track.
Do not harden your heart to them.
Be as you always have been to them, their loving father,
and your mind and heart will be at ease.
Know that you did nothing wrong by loving them all the same.

By Choice

I have seen my girls grow up before my eyes. I have seen them go from making mud pies and playing with dolls to playing with real dolls of their own.   I have cried tears of sadness because I could not give them all the things that a father dreams of giving his children.

I did cry at their weddings when they came to get me and told me it was time.

Already, all too soon.

Dad, it is time.

I did cry when I walked down the aisle with their arms on mine feeling proud to have lived long enough to see them get married. I have cried tears when I heard that they were with child. I have cried tears of blood at just the thought of losing one of them.

But all this I have kept within me for I did not know how to tell them without making them feel heartbroken. So I just kept it in my own aching heart.

But we as Fathers do cry in our own solitude and some of us do pray in our own way for the happiness of our children. Because after all, we are human and we do care for the happiness of our children.

I did become a father by choice and not by chance.

© Ruben Dozal Jr.   9/28/99

Caring People

People in blue, people in white, yelling.
The person on the bed crying,
"Help! Help!"
Total confusion.
"Are you allergic to any medication?"
"Where do you hurt?"
"Can you squeeze my hand?"
"Do you have insurance? What kind?"
And people inside and out, some cry:
The good news that their loved one is okay.
Yet others cry out of grief
For the loss of their loved one.
It all happens in the hospital's emergency ward.
Where colors do not matter,
Where in some cases neither does money.
Rich or poor, people on both sides are the same.
For many days I was one on the outside,
Hoping, praying that my mother would be okay.
And thanks to the hospital staff
And many days of care,
She is doing better. Thank God.
But the prayers are still said
Until she comes home.
Thank you, hospital personnel,
From the bottom of my heart.

©By Ruben Dozal Jr. 4/20/98

11

Congratulations

Congratulations, you have come a long way to see this date.

You see, it paid off, all the hard work, all the homework, all the yelling and screaming of people telling you to do your homework.

People encouraging you to stay in school. Now the day is here and there you are sitting there with your graduation gown on among the few who will get their diplomas today and the very first in your family to graduate from high school.

Yes, the son of poor farm workers, to do it all the way. Yes, take it and live it to its fullest for this day belongs to you and the guts you had to see it through to the end.

The next step will come in due time.

Keep the light on in your mind and the fire in your heart to succeed in life. And make no mistake about it, you will _Succeed._

© Ruben Dozal Jr. 6/10/99

Day Dream

If you only knew my love how much I miss you and hunger for your touch so soft and tender.

Please, Please, my dear sweetheart hear my lonely and sad plea of a lover's humble words.

This is the sadness of a lonely heart that is on fire and my arms, which are hurting in anticipation of holding your warm body close to mine.

Come and fulfill my everyday daydream with a soft kiss my beautiful window lover.

© Ruben Dozal Jr. 12/8/98

Different Roads

Well my friend, it is time to take our own different roads and seek our destinies.

May you find your steps enlightened as you go forth on your new adventure.

We will all miss your smile that would light up a room and your sense of humor, which kept everyone on their toes.

Hope your dreams come true. And do not forget to look up for your guiding Angel that will be smiling at you to.

© Ruben Dozal Jr. 10/12/98

Easy My Love

What time can I see you my love, for I hunger for your touch?

When can I hold you close to me for I miss your warm hand in mine?

When can I see your parents so that we don't have to hide anymore?

Will you not give me an answer little flower of mine?

Easy my love. We still have a lot of time for I am ten and you are only nine.

Empty Home

I wish that I could tell you that since you left everything has been all right. I cannot.

I wish that I could tell you that the pain of the heart is over. I cannot.

I wish that I could tell you that I am having a good time. I cannot.

I wish that I could tell you that I do not miss your smile your walk, which always drove me crazy just to see you move so gracefully. I cannot.

I wish that I could tell you all these things, but when I open the door to our empty house I fall apart because I expect to see you again. And my heart starts to feel heavy once again and my eyes also start to get watery just thinking that I had it all and lost it because of my _Jealousy_.

© By Ruben Dozal Jr. 2/24/99

False Love

Why do you not just walk away from my life?

For the promises you made to me were false.

The kisses you gave me were without feeling.

And the nights we spent together were nothing but a game to you.

I gave you my love freely and you took it and played with it like a baby's toy.

Go, get away from me, and just leave for I cannot see you again.

For the day that I see you again I might beg you to stay.

© *By Ruben Dozal Jr.   1/19/99*

1998

Nineteen Ninety- eight, has been a year of sorrow to both of our families. First, my wife's cousin passed away, Followed by my sister's murder at the hands of her own son with two shots to the heart, which ended her life instantly. Then my wife's aunt passed away due to a heart attack. Then another cousin passed away due to liver problems.

Then on Saturday, November 14th, my mother passed away which has really made me think: is this the way it should be, or what's the hurry?

I have to stop more often to see and enjoy the blessings of our Heavenly Father.

For I know the pain that I carry within me at this time that is tearing me apart just thinking of my mother's passing away.

It seems to me that the more I try not to think about it, the worse it gets.

So again I ask of you my all mighty God to help me find peace of mind and help me find my way back to the living, for I feel empty and lonesome.

I feel that I am living, but not understanding why. I am moving, but in slow motion, so it looks like.

It is time to start to live again and live again I will try to, so help me God.

© Ruben Dozal jr. 12/24/98

Don't Lie Son

"Oh my son, how much more time will I be here in the hospital? I do not see myself getting any better. My legs are weak, my movements are getting slower, and my eyesight is getting worse, tell me...do not lie to me...my son." "Please no lies."

When she said this, my throat became dry, I could not speak, my eyes got watery, and my chest felt heavy. I reached out, held her hand, and told her the truth about what was happening. "You have diabetes and everything in your body is slowing down. Dialysis is not making your body any better."

She looked at me in a manner unlike any other from the past. She said, "The end is near for me my son."

"When do I go home, please tell me, when do I go home." My mother cried. I tried, but could not hold back any longer. With our hands held, my eyes cried with tears of sorrow and anguish. My heart ached and felt like it was coming out of my chest. All I could say was "soon madre Mia."

With that, I took her back to her room. Her glazed eyes spoke to me, "please son, take me home." I told myself, "I will take you home my loving mother, so that you may enjoy the sunrise, the laughter of my grandchildren, and the cool breeze of the wind."

I love you Madresita Mia.

© *by Ruben Dozal Jr.*

Esse

Esse, what are you doing here?

Esse vato, you know that you are on the wrong side of town? And the fighting would start before you had a chance to say another word just because you lived on the other side of town.

Those were some of the things that I had to put with just to see some of my friends from school, when I had the time to try and see them. But most of the time I didn't because of my work.

I would get in a fight when I would go to the store for my mother or my father. It did not make any difference what store I would go to because all the stores were out of our area, just a couple of blocks away. But it did not matter. All they saw was that I did not live close by. That's all, and the fighting would start. Most of the time I was the loser because of my size, which was small and skinny.

I remember one day my mother sent me to the store in the morning to get milk and eggs. I thought, okay, it is still early and I could make it before anybody would see me, yeah.

But I was wrong; I made it home with a box of scrambled eggs and a half carton of milk on my head.

Well, I thought to myself, at least I did not get beat up this time like before.

As time went by that word ESSE was a signal to put up your hands and prepare to fight.

Oh, and by the way, I did become a good fighter.

© By Ruben Dozal Jr. 8/10/99

First Smile

Yours was the first smile I saw.

Yours was the first greeting that I received.

You were the first person that took an interest in my past work history and took the time to listen to me. Things like that you do not forget so easy.

You always gave me a smile when you walked by. You never turned your face at me, and for that I thank you because you made me feel for the first time in my life that I was part of a company.

I hope that your retirement will keep you in good health and that the smile will never leave you.

God Bless You.

Always your friend, Ruben

© Ruben Dozal Jr. 3/23/99

Getting Home

On a cool and beautiful night a woman walks home from the show. As she goes across the park she hears footsteps so she starts to go a little faster. Then she hears another set of footsteps. Now there are two, so her steps get quicker trying to get to the safety of her home across the park. She starts to say to herself, *please help me God*. Then another set of footsteps is heard.

By this time she is ready to yell so it seems. Instead she sees the light of the park. *Light* she thinks. If I can get there I will be all right. Please just a little bit more. When she trips and looks back, the three dark figures are right behind her. She reaches the park light, sits on the bench, and then seconds later the three strangers approach her.

Hi there pretty one. You sure were walking fast sweetie.

The only thing she said *was, please do not hurt me because I am with child.*

What kind of talk is that, I am with child? Yes, you are going to be with child all right after we get done with you.

Please do not hurt me, I beg of you.

The laughter just got louder from them.

Help me dear God, just help me!

With that she knelt down in front of the bench. She put her hands to her face and told them again. *Please do not hurt me,* but in the laughter the three young men did not hear her.

Moments later three young men lie breathlessly looking up to the sky with the reflection of the shining stars in their still eyes.

Good Morning

Good Morning,
Yeah, what's good about it!
You're Alive!

Go see the rising sun over the hills,
That is the beginning of a new day.

The birds singing, the darkness slowly
giving way to the light of a new day.

Adventure is waiting for you.
A new challenge waiting to be conquered as you go forth to do the task
at hand and remember,
It is a Good Morning and my God

I AM ALIVE!

© By Ruben Dozal Jr. 4/18/98

Grandpa's Hair

Grandpa, how come you do not have hair?

Because when you were born you did not have any
And grandma took mine off and gave it to you girls!

Oh, so that's why we have some, ha? Yes!

Are you girls going to give it back to me? No grandpa!

Why not?

Because then we won't have any grandpa. That why Grandpa!

© By Ruben Dozal Jr. 8/28 /98

Family in Need

Once again I come to you, my all-merciful God in Heaven and ask that you straighten out your hand and help my daughter and her husband rekindle the wonders of love again.

To look upon each other the way they did before with love and respect. And for their new life which will be the true testimony of togetherness and harmony for the sake of the family.

Soften their hearts once again for one another so they can see and feel each others' heart according to your will and that they will understand the help of thy mighty hand.

Thank you my God in Heaven.

Your servant, Amen.

© By Ruben Dozal Jr. 8/15/99

Fantastic Night

We had a fantastic time together. I loved every minute of it, yes I did. But there is one thing wrong, because you did not.

We shared our love physically but your heart and love were not there.

Why do you play with the hearts of love so cruelly and coldly?

It seems that love is not in your heart to give freely but for a prize.

Be careful because the revenge of love can be painful, very painful, especially when you ignore it.

© Ruben Dozal Jr. 6/11/99

Fever Talk

Do not cry for me my son for I have lived a good life full of surprises. Full of wonders and full of love for my children, and your father who is waiting for me now.

Please let me rest next to him. Will you promise me, will you promise me my son?
"Yes, Okay AMA, but rest now."
Okay, Okay.

Looking up in the emergency room to the ceiling, maybe from the fever that she had of 104.4 and then 105.5, she started to pray.

You know that I am ready my dear Lord. Why my God, why do you not hear me and end this suffering for me so that my son can enjoy his life.

© By Ruben Dozal Jr.   7/11/98

Final Word

In the early morning hours of the day as we leave our homes to work and our minds become engaged in the work of the day, we stop thinking about our family troubles sometimes.

But when work gets to you and your judgments become cloudy, I like to think of running water, mountains, deer, and birds, anything at the moment. Or words or actions that my grand-daughters have put me through. Because after all, you do control your sanity and the final word.

©Ruben Dozal Jr. 6/6/99

First Kiss

Can I walk with you?
Okay.

Can I carry your books?
Yes, thank you.

What's your name?
Linda.

And what's yours?
Frank.

Well Frank, thank you, but we are at my room.
Already?

Yes, and can I please have my books back?
Oh, I am sorry, here.

See you, see you later.

So I walked away like I was floating on air thinking I have finally found
a girl that did not turn me down. Finally, yeah!
After four months of seeing this beautiful girl finally I had the nerve to
ask her out. And the answer was yes!
I was so excited about the date that I did not want anything to go wrong.
And when I saw her all dressed up my eyes were about to come out of
their sockets and my tongue flew out of my mouth because my girl had
turned into a beautiful butterfly. She made me so very happy just to hold
her hand and be able to go out with her. We had a good time at the dance
all night because it seemed like I was dancing on the clouds of love. But
the dance was over that quick.
When I took her home still with my head in the clouds, without warning
she gave me a kiss. My first kiss and I thought that I was going to melt

29

away by the feeling that my body felt and my lips, which I thought, had fallen off.
I said good night and walked home, because I forgot about my car.

© *By Ruben Dozal Jr.   9/1/99*

Forbidden Fruit

"Husband, where is your wife?"
"I know not."
"Husband, where is she that loves you so deeply and cares for you?"
I say again, "I know not, for I broke her heart with another."

"Husband, will you not at least try to find her?"
"No, I cannot. For I am dying of shame."
"Husband, it is bad enough that you have tasted the forbidden fruit and found it to be bitter, for not harvesting from your own tree. The taste will be with you for a long time to come. But the tree will give another new crop of fruit and this time it will satisfy your hunger."

"Husband, go look for your wife and harvest the new fruit together."
"I know not where to look."
"Open the door to your Home."

© by Ruben Dozal Jr.   1/25/99

Forgiveness Not

Congratulations, you have finally won the war.

Congratulations, look what you have done to me, for I cannot eat or sleep.

Congratulations, for you were right in telling me that you were in my heart forever and that you never were going to leave until I would come to my knees and beg for forgiveness.

Congratulations, for the reflections of you that follow me everywhere I look, in windows, mirrors, and pieces of glass. Any reflection brings your smile to my eyes.

Congratulations, for I feel my life slowly slipping away just the same way you told me it would.

Congratulations, for the final sleep is at hand but forgiveness not.

© Ruben Dozal Jr. 6/5/99

Get Out

It was Saturday morning and I was the first to wake up. By this time it was about 80 degrees outside, so I put my shorts on and went out to play. To my surprise I saw an eight-foot gopher snake, so I caught it and put it around my waist under my shirt.

As the day went by I did not think much of it that I had the snake. Then in the afternoon I went to the store across the street to get an ice cream. That was my bad, bad, bad mistake because I forgot about the snake around my waist.

I was paying for the ice cream when the snake pulled its head out from under my shirt and all chaos broke loose!

The lady at the counter cursed me out and told me if she ever saw me in the store again that she was going to call the police and have them take me away. Then she told me to get out! Out! And not to come back again.

So I did, but I left the snake.

Ù
© Ruben Dozal Jr.   7/31/98

Chicken

I fear for the light of day for it will disrupt our night of passion.

It will be time to face the enemy and we both know that they are without mercy.

Trying all the time to get the best of us no matter what we try to do for them. It is always the same answer, "You do not understand us."

It is time.
"No not yet. Stay a little more time."
"I cannot for I fear for my sanity."
Here they come.

"Mom, Dad, where are you?"
"Good-bye and good luck."
Chicken, Chicken!!
Ù

© By Ruben Dozal Jr.   1/27/99

Cold Night

The nights have been cold
although I cover myself, my body,
still yearn for the warm and soft touch of your body close to mine.

Maybe it was your fault or mine for the fight we had, but who cares. Just
come so that we can start up the fire again.

Ù

© by Ruben Dozal Jr. 2/9/99

Daddy's Angel

The doorbell rings. The woman upstairs hurries down to open it. *My God, who can it be at this time of the night*? But before she opens the door she looks through the peephole and outside stands a well dressed man. So she asks, *Who is it?* The man answers, *it concerns your children*. The woman opens the door right away. The stranger comes in, slowly looks around a bit, then the mother, carrying a gun in her night coat pocket, asks, *Yes, what about my children?* The stranger answers, *where are they now mother?* Upstairs in their rooms asleep. Well they better be there, I mean. Not saying another word she turns and runs upstairs. She opens the first door, then the other door. The rooms were empty.

She screams and cries in terror, runs downstairs to talk to the stranger, but she sees no one around. So she goes to the phone to call for help. By the phone she sees a note that read, *go to the park Mother, but leave your gun at home. There you will be gratified.* So she opens the drawer by the phone, puts the gun down, and runs out of the house to the park. There hugging each other and crying were her children. All they said looking up to the heavens,

"We were just trying to see the Angels that took Daddy, Mommy."

© by Ruben Dozal Jr. 6/25/98

Dialysis Personnel

Day in, day out the gratitude that I feel for you dialysis people is over-whelming.

For if it was not for your caring and helping my mother in her last days, I feel that I might have lost her a long time ago.

I thank you for the extra time you made it possible for me to hold her close to me, to hear her voice, and to love her the only way that a son can love his Mother. And do not forget that a smile from one of you might lighten up a smoldering candle.

Do not forget just a smile.

© BY Ruben Dozal Jr. 1/30/99

Enjoy It

You are getting ready for another adventure in your life. May I say that I had my eyes on you, but not as a spy but as one that did not want anything to happen to you because you have been a good friend to me.

At times a little unstable, a little outspoken, and at times a little strange especially when you are making a blend, with chemicals but nevertheless a friend and I am going to miss you.

I hope that when my time comes to pull the plug I would be full of energy like you. And be able to say, "I made it!"

"I made it!"

God blesses you and enjoy it.

© By Ruben Dozal Jr. 2/5/99

Anticipation

Have I become so old, so cold, as to not see or feel the sensation?
Of my poor rapid heartbeat when you come close to me.
The fresh smell of your body when you come out of the shower.
 The sweet woman - scent that drives me crazy with anticipation of our next move.
 Come lie by me and maybe, just maybe, I am not that old after all.

© by Ruben Dozal Jr. 2/10/99

At Last

You have given me love without a price.
You have kept the fire burning like a torch in my heart.
You have taken all the burdens from my shoulders and put them on yours without saying a word, nothing at all.
You have given my children your name without regret.
You have given up your freedom for my six children and me and now they call you father. In what words can I say I, I, Love you?
Sometimes man cannot live alone and feel free. All my life I wondered what it would be like and feel like inside when little ones call you Father or my Wife tells me I love you. Now I have both

38

and will not trade that for anything in the world, my beloved wife.

The good Lord has really smiled and blessed me. Thank you with all my heart. Just do not stop Loving me.

© By Ruben Dozal Jr. 2/11/99

BOY IN NEED

For many days now I have been trying very hard to stay away from my parents. I don't want them to ask me questions about the jacket and tennis shoes they bought me for my birthday. I know that sooner or later they are going to ask me, what happened to them? I am trying very hard to make up a story that they will believe, or should I tell the truth? Either way I am going to be in deep trouble.

I decided to tell them the truth — when no sooner — they asked me the question, "Where is the jacket and tennis shoes we bought you for your birthday?" asked my mom and dad. I told them I gave them to a needy person.

" You did WHAT!" yelled my dad.

"Yes, I gave them away to a needy person." I told my dad. My dad looks at my mom and says, " you talk to him." But then he decided that he would talk to me. "Son, your mother and I paid a lot of money for those things." My dad said.

"Yes, I know."

I looked at my mom and said, "But mom, this person did not have any shoes or jacket and it was very cold outside. I just gave them to him."

My dad told me, "Son, you just don't give those kinds of things away, especially to a black boy."

I told my dad, "He was white, and very in need."

My dad yelled out, "WHAT WHITE! Now I know you have really lost your mind."

He told me to go to bed and he would never buy me anything for a long time. He also told me I better not even come and ask him for anything.

A terrible feeling of sadness came to my heart as I went to my bedroom. This feeling came because I felt my parents did not understand me.

One year came and went since that dreadful day. Another six months passed. It is now Christmas time.

On Christmas morning a box arrives with my name on it.

"What a surprise, who would be sending me something." I thought to myself. Maybe it was my mom or dad?

I ran to ask them why they would send me a box through the mail. After I asked them, all they could say was, "what box?" Mom and dad ran beside me to go open the box. I started to open it when I noticed there was no note or card inside to see who had sent it.

As I took the cover off I was shocked to see my jacket and tennis shoes, just like new. I searched for a note, but had no luck, still nothing.

When I put one of my shoes on I hit my toe on something.

I put my hand inside and pulled out a key. Attached to the key was a note.

The note said, "Thank you for helping me in my time of need. There are still some good young people in this old beautiful world. Sometimes the good deeds are the ones that get bypassed by the bad ones. Your Guiding Angel, it was with you on that day. You helped me, without even thinking about the outcome you would have with your parents. That took a lot of courage. Now take the key which shows you my gratitude."

The address was in the other shoe with a note that read, " The house that opens with this key belongs to you and your family."

All I could do was yell. Mom-Dad-Dad-Mom-Mom!

© Ruben Dozal Jr. on July 27, 1998.

Getting Papers

What are you doing here? You speak English? Are you going to school?
You have your family here? Then why are you working like us?
Because, like you, I need money for school and to help my mother and
father.
But you are so young.
Yes, I am.
How old are you?
I lied, eighteen, but I had just turned fifteen. And you, how old are you?
I am forty-six. And what brings you here? Work and money, always the
same answers.
Do you have a family?
Yes, all in Mexico. I was an accountant in Mexico and I worked for the
biggest bank there. Why are you working here then?
Because I am trying to get money so I can get my papers right and bring
my family here with me.
Do you miss them? Tears just started coming down his cheeks.
Yes, I do young man, yes, I do.
With that I gave him a hug and we both cried.

Ù
© Ruben Dozal Jr.   1998

41

Hear The Sound

Oh, my dear, hear the sound of a new life it is so precious, so sweet and so innocent. This is a testimony of our Love that we share.

The good Lord has made our lives complete now. You to me and I to you.

Hear, listen to the tender sounds of your son and that the Love we have will never die. I truly believe that our Love has just been given another tremendous spark of life.

And I do Love you.

© By   Ruben Dozal Jr. 1/30/99

I Saw You

"Where have you been?" It is late, you told me that you were going to wait for me, that you had something important to tell me. Instead you are late and you know that I hate it when you are late.

And you come like nothing was going on, as if you were not late at all. Spare me the details you cheat.

"What? Cheat? Why do you talk to me like this?"

"Like if you did not know."

"Do not play games with me. I saw you with another in my house today, yes I was there. I went to get my tennis shoes upstairs."

"But, but, you do not understand."

"What do I do not understand? Was it the embracing and the kiss that I saw, or did I not see it?

"This is very hard to explain to you. Wait, wait, please do not hit me, no please stop, stop! But no words were heard."

Later at the hospital the other man shows up with fire in his eyes, looking, looking for something to grab, but instead just jumps at his face and the other man grabs him tight not letting him go and asks,

"Is my sister okay?"

© By Ruben Dozal Jr.   2/17/99

Look at me

Beautiful lady, so fine, so high class, every time you walk by my heart picks up another beat and the thought of having you just goes wild in this poor mind of mine.

But it cannot be, because you belong to another. But even so, maybe a word or two someday that I might hear from your luscious lips would make me feel like a king.

Beautiful lady, I wish that I could ask what is bothering you because of the sadness in your eyes that tells the story of unhappiness now for a while.

Beautiful lady, will you not lower your sights upon me so that I might help you, if only once?

Beautiful lady, the sunset is giving way to the night and the cool breeze feels good on my boiling body. Now is the hardest time. I think of you and the dreams become so real that I can no longer take it.

Beautiful lady, my lady.

Hi.

Excuse me.

© By Ruben Dozal Jr. 4/5/99

Lost Power

Hey! What are you doing you are making a mess there is nothing for you there: Now pick everything up and put it back in the trash. Don't you have any shame?

The man turned and said, yes I do have shame, but shame does not feed an empty stomach nor does it put clothes on my back. Yes I do have shame, but do not feel sorry for me. Just help if you can but do not feel sorry for I have had it all. And lost it all because of my drug use and my drinking and for that I lost it all.

43

As he got closer something told me that the face looked familiar. But I could not place it because of the dirt and beard he had on his face. As he talked more I knew who he was but did not say anything. I felt just like reaching out and grabbing him and walking all over him.

This was the same man who got me fired by saying lies about me and my work just to gain power.

So I just listened for awhile and gave him something to eat and some money. As he walked away he stopped turned, put his hand in the air and said thank you. "I am sorry" and called me by my name.

© By Ruben Dozal Jr.   3/5/99

Mis Ojos

To mis ojos hold your self in tack for the power of the Lord has not for sanken you. But his mighty hand has been put out to help you do not turn your face from it but hold on tight and the answered will revel its self to you.

Keep your head up in pride and dignity for you have a long road to go and the obstacles are hidden from sight so go very carefully but do not loose the grip on who is helping you.

Please be aware of all the love that is all around you. The beautiful little faces that look at you and ask for your help. Love and a smile is their reward for you helping them, which will travel to the deepness of your heart forever.

Please, please, do not harden your heart against them for they are so precious and so innocent for in them the only weapon they carry is love and a smile.

©By Ruben Dozal Jr. 8/6/99

My Dear and Beloved Brother,

Why do you not see your hands in front of you, are they not the same?

So is the love of the rest of our family - do not ease them

44

out. They hunger and feel just like you. They also feel the pain of your sons, which at this moment is tearing you apart inside.

Fear not for them at this moment for the hand of
the Lord is with you and them.

You have given love and kindness to them.
You have taught them right from wrong and the difference between good and evil.

The rest is up to them to decide.
They have to choose and experience the fruits of their choosing alone.

Look beyond the final trial. Do not harden your heart to
them. Be as you always have been to them, their loving
father, and your mind and heart will be at ease. Know that you did not do nothing wrong by loving them all the same.

Your brother,
Ruben Dozal Jr.

©By Ruben Dozal Jr. 8/6/98

<u>My Dear Sister,</u>

Why do you hate or dislike mother so much, you have built a wall so high that no one can climb it without getting hurt. No one can talk to you without getting into a fight. I respect your wishes of letting you live your own way and being left alone, but at least have a heart and call mother even though it hurts you to talk to her. Come and see her, even if for that last time. Relax I do not have anything to tell you that has not already been said. Mother will always love you and she never stops thinking about you. She is always asking if you have called or if you have been here. The answer is always the same, "No mom, I have not heard from her." Then she asks again, "What did I do to her for her not to love me? How come she never calls me?" Then mother starts to cry. All I can tell her is that you did not do anything mom, nothing at all.
So if you have a chance come and see her before death closes her eyes for the last time.

Your brother,

Ruben Dozal Jr.
September 14, 1998

My Grandmother

I never knew my grandmother or my grandfather, but some of the stories that my mother would tell me about them make me sad that I did not know them at all. Especially one of many stories that stands out the most in my memory.

She would tell me that my grandfather was a dead eye with a colt 45 and when they traveled from Qasave to Tesila it would take more than a week or so to get there. But on the way they would camp out wherever the sun would set. And that grandfather would tell them to gather up wood for the fire so that grandma could cook dinner, which was done quickly, and without any back talk because grandpa was a man of all men without fear of anything at all.

My mother would tell me that sometimes in the early morning hours, she could hear gunfire. And that grandma would tell them, "hurry, get up, your father is bringing breakfast" and we would get up and have the fire going by the time grandfather would show up with a rabbit or two al- ready skinned and cleaned just ready for the fire which always tasted good.

Mother also told me that my grandfather had a real bad temper. And one morning when he went hunting for breakfast she heard too many shots, so when grandfather got back grandmother asked him what happened because she had heard so many shots. Grandpa got up and just started yelling at my grandma, saying if you think that you can do better then why didn't she go out in the morning and get breakfast herself. The more he yelled the angrier he got. Finally she turned to grandpa and said, "End this right now." So grandpa got furious and told my two brothers to set up some rocks because grandma and he were going to have a shoot-out.

Mother said that they were all afraid because they had never seen grandma shoot a gun before, even though she always carried one.

Everything was ready and grandpa was loading his Forty-Five and then grandma got there wearing her side Forty-Five never like that before.

Grandpa told grandma the rocks on the right side are yours and the ones on the left side are mine. Okay? And when I count to three we will draw and start to fire. Ready, and my mother said that they got back all the way out of the way because like she said before they had never seen grandma shoot. Then grandpa said one, two, three, and they drew their guns. Grandma knocked all the stones off and part of grandpa's off also. Mother then said that we did not even see her pull the gun out, that's how fast she was, but said that grandpa always knew, and she never missed one shot.

My mother would tell me that grandma was so soft spoken and

that her voice would float like the whispers of the wind, and that she would always call guns the instruments of the devil.

© by Ruben Dozal Jr. 2/21/99

New Life

As you go forth with a new life, within you your seed will continue and your love will be renewed for the life you are going to hold in your hands was conceived out of Love.

Fear not for the God above has sent an Angel to watch over you both.

Love and Happiness to you both,

© By Ruben Dozal Jr. 9/11/98

Nido Y Masita

One part of my life has ended; the other ended in nineteen eighty-five. The memories of them both will burn and burn forever and ever with in me until the good Lord closes my eyes for all time.

They are both together now in a warm embrace looking down upon us saying, "They will be alright I know."

Hold my hand, my beloved Nido and walk with me.
O.k. Masida and let them fine happiness.

© Ruben Dozal Jr 3/15/99

No Answer

"Who are you?" A man asked me as I walked around my work area. I answered him with the same question.
The man replied, "I am an engineer and I am here to see how our new condenser is working."

All I said, "Okay," and I left. An hour later I came back and the engineer was still sitting there in the same place looking at the machine.

So he told me, "You know, I have been looking at this machine you have here and I cannot figure out how in the world it works."

"Okay," I answered him, "if you like I can explain it to you. That is, if you have time."

"Please do," he replied. So after about an hour of explaining the machine to him, he asked me, "Who runs the machine now?" "I do," I told him.

"You really must have had a lot of schooling to run this machine."

I could not answer. Than he told me whoever put this machine together had his work cut out for him. And I still could not answer him, because it would take a man with a lot of talent to do it.

Then he thanked me for explaining the working of the machine to him.

"Oh, I am sorry, what is your name?"

"I am the builder of the machine," I answered.

"Then you must have a degree in engineering?"

All I could say was, "I have to go."

How could I tell him that I did not even finish High School.

© By Ruben Dozal Jr. 1/27/99

No More, Dad

Oh my dear father, why do you Drink so much?

Why do you hurt so deeply, for I can see your sorrow?

Open your eyes and see what you have done to me. Look at the bruises on my body that you have left on it. Do you not love me for I surely love you? Look at me my father now that you have not started to drink yet.

Feel my tears of sadness dear father coming down my checks. Feel my hand shake when I stretch it out to touch yours.

Please my dear father, hear my words and do not hit me anymore. Yes, that's what I am going to tell him when I get out of the hospital this time, I will tell him, yes I will.

© 1/1/99 by Ruben Dozal Jr.

No Problem

Boy, how do you do it?

Do what?

Well, everytime I see you, you are so cheerful and happy with no problems in your mind at all, no problems.

Listen to this. My wife is having an affair with another, no problem.

My children are having children with no father to be seen, no problem. My son alone has three with no wife, no problem.

They come and go as they please. My house is in shambles, no law, no respect for my laws or me but no problem.

The only real problem is me breathing the air of life, that is all, just breathing but, hay no _problem._

© Ruben Dozal Jr. 6/12/99

Not Forgotten

I Hope and pray that your illness is subsiding, and that you are getting stronger. Please do not think that I have forgotten about you.

Because I have not nor has my humble silent prayer that you get better.

See you Soon.

Your Student,

RUBEN.   ©
BY RUBEN DOZAL JR. 3/2/99

Office Language

Let the light of the day put a smile on your face and speed on your fingers and patience in your tone of voice after you have all of this, OH....I forgot and calmness' let the games begin but the first rule is keep your sanity.

> Maria call extension 200..........
>> Ruben call extension 200..........
>> Whoever answers call extension 200..........

" Did you order the bulk load ? "

" NO ! I thought you did. "

But, but O.K. did you call this customer back.
(face hair up at end, eyes rolling back, lips moving not saying nothing)

"Oh, put these papers in the right file."
(turning around lips still going not saying nothing)

" O.K. "

And here I come to make the day complete. "Can I order parts ?"

" NO ! NO ! I SAID NO ! "

© r dozal jr. 7/2/98

Old MacDonald

"Hi, Grandpa!"
"Hi, girls."
"Did you girls have a good day?"
"Yes, Grandpa."
"No fighting?"
"No, Grandpa."
"No biting?"
"No, Grandpa."
"No kicking?"
"We told you already, we had a nice day Grandpa."
"Did you girls sing a song?"
"We sang Old MacDonald."
"Old MacDonald had what? Three brats?"

Laughing and giggling, "No Grandpa, silly
Grandpa, Old MacDonald had a farm Grandpa."

<u>One Time Lover</u>

I know that I did wrong.

I know that I did lie.

I know that I did cheat.

But that's not why I am here. I am here to beg for your forgiveness.
Because all that I did wrong is choking me out of breath and I indeed feel
the pain now of a broken heart.

So please, please do not turn your face from me but open your heart and
soften it once more, my dear love.

What is your answer, tell me now, please do not take too long to tell me,
what is it?

When it rains with no clouds in the sky, and the river flows up, then I will
take you back, my one time lover.

© By Ruben Dozal Jr. 3/9/99

<u>Suffering Mother</u>

Their once lived a woman with five children
whom she loved more than her own life.
She taught them right from wrong,
The difference between good and evil.
She taught them to love each other.
With words of kindness she taught her children.
The words were never taken to heart because their
Hearts were there but their minds were someplace else.

Day in and day out the woman never gave up
fighting for them. Needless to say, the children
never fought for her. Pain and suffering were her
reward for loving her children so much. Even
with Lupus, she never gave up. Sometimes
she would lie in her bed for a week at a time.
Pale and sick she would drive over hundreds
of miles for treatment one way and back. Tired
and sick she would go out and see the fields to
see what they needed. Not even her sickness
could keep her down for a long time. But a bullet, not one but two, from
a gun in her sons hand put her in the grave.
I loved this woman.   <u>She was my sister.</u>

©By Ruben Dozal Jr. 8/10/98

<u>Sweet Dates</u>

I will start by saying that my life in the sixties was normal, and
to me normal was swimming in the irrigation canals when the canals
were full to irrigate the fields around my home. Climbing date trees was
an art to go up to get the sweet dates, but getting down was another
story. I remember one climb in particular.

It was early morning. I was walking alongside a ditch bank when
I saw the most beautiful dates. I had to have them no matter what, so I
started climbing and about half way up one of the stubs broke. I slid
down a little bit but I found another stub and continued upwards. When
I got to the top I started to cut the date limbs. I think I cut four anyway.
When I got ready to go down, and not looking where to grab, I put my
hand right on one of the palm thorns that almost went through the other
side of my hand. I was trying to push myself up to undo my hand. I stuck
myself in the leg with another thorn, but I could not let go because I was
about fifty feet high, crying, hungry and scared. After I pulled my hand
loose I still could not move, so I stayed in that date tree for about six
hours.

The bad thing about this was that no one knew where I was. The
date tree was away from the road and away from my house. After crying
for awhile, I decided to go down again. This time my legs and hands
were working together. When I finally got down I looked like I had been
in a fight or two.

Then I started home. I forgot about the dates, but my mother did
not forget about me. My mother's special weapon was the broomstick

and the mop stick. I could never outrun them. Well, she broke the broom-stick on me and she was on a roll, no stopping. That woman next came with the mop stick. After a few rights and lefts she let me go and said, "Wait until your father gets home."

After awhile she called me out to go feed the dog.

" O.K. mom," I tried to answer her, but by this time I was all black and blue from her blows. She took one good look at me and said, "what happened to you?"

"Mom, you did this to me."

" Well, you made me mad. Where were you anyway?"

"I went to get some dates, mom. Then I showed her my hands and legs all covered with little holes from the thorns of the palm tree.

"Well, why did you not tell me son? Where are the dates?"

"I left them there mom. Are you going to tell dad?"

"We will see."

© By Ruben Dozal Jr 7/27/98

<u>Taken Away</u>

One afternoon my fellow workers and I had just finished moving sprinkler pipe and we were going back to the main ranch when out of know nowhere the border patrol stopped us.

I was driving the tractor and the other two were on the trailer. The officers asked us in Spanish, "Do you have papers?"

"Yes," they said, "but they are at the house at the ranch." So they told them to get in. Then one officer asked me the same question and I told them "no," so he told me to get in the van, so I did. When they took the other two to the ranch to get their papers they asked me from what part of Mexico I came from.

Then I told them that I was from here. The two officers got pretty unhappy with me when I told them that. "Are trying to be funny with us? "No," I said, "you asked me in Spanish if I had papers, and I said no. Did I not say that?" "Yes you did." "But you did not ask me where I was born at or nothing else."

All they told me was get out get out and don't do this again."

The faces they made at me were enough to know that they where going to be back. And back they did come. But this time they did take some people with them, and when they stopped by us the faces and fears seemed like they were telling us, "help us help us." This really made me see the real meaning of being a Mexican, and without papers.

Ten Years Ago

The night is cool. Remember my little flower when we ran to each other's arms after being away for so long?
The fragrance of your body almost knocked me over. And the perfume on your neck put me in the seductive mood of passion.

Yes, it was a night like this.

But do not forget that we never made it back home to your boyfriends house. It's been ten years now. And the flame is still on.

So it is, so it is.

Come rest by me, put your head on my chest and listen to my heartbeat. Let it be a reminder of how much I love you, my sweet little flower.

By Ruben Dozal Jr. 1/19/99

Thank You

When the early morning clock makes its noise and breaks the sleep of the night, I give thanks to you.

When the feet touched the cold floor as I make my way to the bathroom to get ready for work, I give thanks to you.

When I open the door to the room were I had rested and see the woman of my life, I give thanks to you.

When I look in the other room and see the fruits of our love, I give thanks to you.

When night comes and I see all my family together again and see in the room when they are all a sleep with out a doubt I give thanks to you.

54

That Woman

Come, sit by me , talk to me. What's on your mind?
I am in love , just listen, my friend.
She is the most beautiful woman I have ever seen or spoken with.
Then, what's the problem?
The problem is that she does not know that I am alive.
Yeah, so what's new?
She moves me, excites me and her smile lights up my heart.
Her perfume smells like an ocean breeze.
Yeah! You're in love all right. Does this woman have a name?
Yes, but I do not know it.
Don't get your hopes up.
I am trying not too, but at my age I do not have time for games.
I am afraid that she might turn me down.
Go for it! You fool.
I am going for it tomorrow.
Later that night my friend passed away from a heart attack.
At the funeral I saw the woman he was in love with.
I spoke to her quietly.
I just wanted you to know that he was in Love…in Love with you.
She didn't turn, she just said, I know he was, he was my Father.

© By Ruben Dozal Jr. 4/18/98

The Beast

"Granpa, is the beast tied up?"
"Yes" I told you "why?"
"Because my sisters and I are going to Play outside a little bit O.K."
"But stay in the backyard and pick up your junk when you finish playing O.K."
"O.K. grandpa."
"What did you say?"
"I said, O.K. grandpa."
Than I heard one of the girls say, "granpa likes to yell a lot huh!"
"Why" her sisters answers.
"I think because he is old." "Yeah he's old."
Seconds later—the three little bodies almost knocked me down
All yelling and crying "granpa you lied to us you lied to us"
"The beast is lose and he jumped at us and bit me and he scathed me."
"O.K. O.K. I am sorry."

"No your not your mean and old yes you are grandpa."
"Here, come with me and we will tie him up O.K."
"O.K. grandpa."
"You go" one of the girls tells the other.
"No you go" "no let my little sister go."
O.K. little one lets go tie up the beast
"No grandpa I am scared."
"O.K. grandpa you go."
So I went to tie up the beast and when I got back inside the girls told me, "we rather watch the rug rats grandpa."

© 8/22/1998, by Ruben Dozal Jr.

The Man

To the man that took a chance and gave me a job and let me show some of the skills other wise would have been hidden.

To the man that fought hard to make his dreams come true.

To the man that had all the burdens of a company on his shoulders.

To this man that treated me fair and with respect.

To this man, I say thank you.

I will always keep you in my inner soul forever.

God Bless You.

Thank you,
Ruben

© By Ruben Dozal Jr. 8/30/99

The Eagle

All my life I have worked with pride and dignity tried hard if not harder then anyone else to learn the work that I was supposed to do. Because of that I really thought deep inside it was because of my education that I was bypassed for promotions. Sadly to say, that was not so, but because I was a Mexican.

56

I worked for a company for many years and in that time I was bypassed for promotions about five times, if not more.

I brought myself up through the hard ranks of learning how to work with tractors. Even with chemical test scores higher than anybody else's with my training certificates plus passing the truck driving license and all the endorsements, with all this just to get ahead and I was still bypassed for a promotion. On the truck-driving test I missed only one out of about eighty questions.

I was not even given a chance or asked if I wanted the job as fore man. The company brought in outside men to do the job, but they never, never gave me the chance to try it.

Perhaps it was better that way, because none of them could do the work right anyway.

They would come with the Eagles stuck on their shoulders. The wings would be so wide open that it would seem you needed to help them with the door so that you could see the spender and strength of the Eagle when they came in through the door.

Now it seems that sometimes it starts to feel the same way all over again, because I have to prove what I know and who I am. All over again, and the discrimination starts to show its ugly face once more.

The Eagle has never left; it just changed places and got more educated.

© By Ruben Dozal Jr. 4/11/99

<u>The Surprise</u>

"Help, help, please help me," a young women cries out.
-People walking by not wanting to get involve-
Because of the blows of her assailants-total of three-
The young woman bleeds from her mouth and noise.
The assailants pull the young woman by her hair into the alley.
The assailants try to pull her deeper and deeper into the alley, as one of them trips and tumbles down over an old Wine-o sleeping on the cold

57

wet floor covered with newspapers.

The assailant gets up angry and yells insanities to the poor Wine-o.

In his eyes was the look of terror and hate.

He attacks the poor man while his friends

where pulling the young women deeper into the ally.

The young man without warning attacks the Wine-o.

This time the Wine-o was up,

it did not matter that the attacker kept coming and found

Himself in disbelieve looking up to the sky the attacker looks up and

All around to see if any body saw what happen he sees nothing just the

Wine-o standing up by the wall so his anger is multiplies and continues to

Cause at the old Wine-o and attacks again and again fines himself

Looking up to the sunlight thinking what happen. This time the Wine-o

Was wide-awake but said nothing but could see clearly on what was going

On as his assailant was trying to get up he goes over and hits him one

More time then turns his face and looks at the other two with the face

Of a wolf on a hunt a look that would melt ices and goes after them

With no fear at all so one off them turns around and knocks the girl

Out with one blow he figures they would get back to her after they took

Care of the Wine-o. As both of them came charging the old Wine-o hands

Were moving so fast hitting their faces with no misses and as they pull

Back in shock and look at each other and again came at him more deter-

mine

Then before this time Death was in their eyes but instead surprise was

Their reward for they found them selves beaten up tied up along with

Their other partner. After the fight, the old Wine-o, goes over and helps

the young girl up. He cleans her up a little and just held her hand for

A minute. He Winks his eye and was gone.

© 9/17/98 BY RUBEN DOZAL JR.

<u>The Time Book</u>

Do not be afraid, go ahead and open the book.

Time has truly gone by because you are reading it now, so please read on.

The time is nineteen ninety-nine and man has come a long way in find-ing ways to destroy himself without the help of anybody.

Man has invented airplanes, cars and trains to transport people from place to place.

Computers to further educate ourselves, and telephones to help us communicate with each other.

Yes, we have invented hundreds of wonderful things to help man.

But we have also invented hatred, discrimination, and slavery, and in some places the art of killing people for money or just for fun.

There were many different races on earth or there used to be. Now only memories and legends are left, thanks to our own destruction of mankind.

Look to the heavens and go bend your knees with your loved ones and give thanks to the *All Mighty God* for granting you another day.

I hope and pray that everyone is living in harmony all over the world. And peace, my God peace, has finely conquered the hearts of mankind.

Your great, great-grandfather

© Ruben Dozal Jr. 4/19/99

The Train

I can hear the whistle blowing in the early morning light. Yes, the whistle of the train that is going to take you away from me.

The mournful sound that is getting closer and closer.

The words of saying good-bye are harder and harder to say, but the inevitable reality is here finally on the tracks of steel.

Remember me and the good times we had together. Do not forget to write, write me.

I will not see my love again for I feel it in my heart. Her dream of seeing something different has reached deep inside of her soul and the heat of excitement is dancing all over her luscious body, moving around like a busy bee and my heart sinking deeper and deeper in despair.

It is time. Yes, it is. Look at you ready for the big city?

Oh, yes, I am ready until I see you again.

Yes, maybe, or maybe not.

© Ruben Dozal Jr. 7/8/99

THUNDER IN THE STREET

I heard the thunder, indeed I heard the noise. On both the young and old I saw the different looks on their faces, the excitement in their eyes as the glitter of man and machine drove by.

The young trying just like the old to see which machine was the best looking one.

But for me to see the multitude gather together was a sight to see all kinds of people coming together, not caring about anyone's color or nationality.

Just friendship, that's all. `

© by RUBEN DOZAL JR.   7/4/98

Till Tomorrow

It is hard for me to say goodnight to you because, I fear for the early morning light,
to show me as I look into your room, no movement from your breath.

No warm body to touch
No slow good morning words
No God bless you my son.

I know that your heath is not so good...*but* your mind and words
are still truthful and your *pure love*. That's why I say
Till Tomorrow Ama.

Tiny Hands

The tiny hands that touched me.

The little smile that I saw.

The little eyes that tried to open to the light of day.

The little body that I held in my arms. These are all gifts from our heavenly Father to let us know that my seed will continue.

And that his mighty hand is still with us never to let go, holding on tight for all people to see.

©

By Ruben Dozal Jr. 8/9/99

To My Daughters

You both have filled the emptiness of my heart, and are the reason to prevail and get ahead in life. From the very start you two came into my life, we have not been the same. It is only fitting that I say why I say these things to you now. But first, take a good look around you and be glad for all that you have now, today.

My daughters, when your mother and I got married, we had nothing but each other. Our honeymoon was spent in a 10' by 15' room that was our castle. That was also the saddest time in my life. It was the coldest, chilliest room. There were cracks in the door that would let could wind in at night. We cuddled together to keep warm. When your mother fell asleep, I could feel the tears start to come down my cheeks with no solution in sight.

The bed we had was four apricot boxes put upside down, and I bought an old mattress. We slept good once we got used to it. Yes, my daughters try getting up at night and go to the restroom out side when it is raining. We did not have water inside, no shoes, and not even gas to cook our food with. It was hard, and on top of that, the odds of us making it were two million to one- but I did not give up.

I remember one day that has stayed in my heart like rusty nail with no head, the one you can not pull out. The rain had started with no end in sight and you could not work. We did not have any food or money so we were going to your grandmas to eat. Then the depression set in, and before we crossed the tracks, I, your father, just started crying and crying. Here I was, married and could not even feed your mother much less myself.

My daughters, I tell you this so you will understand that when the good Lord gives and takes away, he does it without mercy. So learn how to live with what you have. Make it work, for now.

My daughters, before my eyes are closed for the last time, I give thanks to you and the good Lord for giving me the chance of being your father.

To MY Young Daughter

Oh my daughter what has live taught you at a young age, because you are trying very hard to be Loved. But love from words does warm a cold heart, but an act of kindness might.

Right now you are at the crossroads, and the directions are all different and you are wearing blind folds and ask by your love ones to show them the way.

The choice that will make you happy is the one you choose and no matter what try to make it your own and stand by it. For your choices will always be hard and difficult because of your little ones. Think my daughter of the out come for what is best for them, but also do not leave yourself out.

Please my daughter do not be so hard on me for the way I talk to your kids for I know deep with in me that I love them and you with all my old Heart.

I am very proud of you and what you have done to help you and your girls. The good Lord will continual to help you long after I am gone put a little Faith in him and see the wonders of his work.

Your Father.

© Ruben Dozal Jr. 12/27/98

To The Future

A Boy goes to school but does not know what the other kids are talking about, so he stays by himself. Yes, in the 50's.

He tries very hard to understand the other kids and it is the start of the struggle that will shape his life forever. Yes, in the 50's.

He keeps going to school and some days he does not want to go because he starts to hear words that he does not understand. Kids make fun of him because he is a greaser. But it is the 50's.

Ha, but in the 60's the boy understands well what the words mean and the fighting begins with himself and others to find his place in the 60's.

War is in full force in Vietnam. Young people are dying to save a country but are slowly being pushed out of the fight and evil is the victor. But it is the 60's.

Flower children are trying to be heard. Racial tension in LA, fire and killing is the answer. But it is the 60's.

Farm workers are united and are heard all over the land and a leader is born. Cesar Chavez was his name. But still, it is only the 60's.

A president arrives in Texas for a visit and leaves in a coffin. His brother arrives for a visit in LA, both by the name of Kennedy. Both are killed in the 60's.

The war keeps on, people are still dying left and right, friends, brothers, fathers never returning to hold their loved ones. But it is only the 70's.

New laws are put down to protect people from themselves. The world is standing to see the end of the war and it does come to an end in the 70's.

New Hope starts to take shape for the lucky ones who served, but the healing will last a lifetime. But it is the 70's.

The world is starting to come to its own, so it seems. Countries are starting to cry for freedom at last in the 80's.

The burden of freedom carries a heavy price indeed for the old and new. The same price is felt in the 80's.

Children or kids having kids is the talk of the day. Son against father, daughter against mother, seems to be growing more common in the 80's.

Gangs and drivebys are talked about freely with no remorse for the dead. How can they have any if they do not even know whom they have killed? But it is only the 80's.

And the wars keep on coming, the poor and homeless cannot see any peace in the 90's.

Millions of people having children to carry out a fight that happened thousands of years ago, but still cannot shake hands and live in peace. But it is only the 90's.

People live and people die and peace still does not ring true in the ears of man. But it is only the 90's.

Planes drop bombs, guns are fired in the night-light, and in the morning everyone is counting their dead. More graves are dug, massive graves that could take upwards of one hundred people who are just pushed in and covered up, never to know the names of the dead. But it is only the 90's.

So my children, these are some of the things that I, your Great Great-Grandfather, have been able to put down on paper for you to read.

I really did not want to scare you, but that's the way it has been in the fifty years that I have lived.

So if you have a chance, gather all your loved ones, bow your heads and bend your knees in prayer to the All Mighty God for not destroying mankind… Yet.

Your Great Great-Grandfather, Ruben Dozal Jr.

© By Ruben Dozal Jr. 4/22/99

<u>To The Reading Program</u>

To the shock of my humble self I thank you for the opportunity of reading some of my work to so many.

To me I did win first prize. That cannot be replaced, not by anything in the world.

To see so many people giving me, a farm worker by trade, a standing ovation by so many beautiful people has really put me in a state of shock.

I thank you for opening the door of knowledge to me and to my beautiful tutor who has had her hands full and patience with me.

Thank you, Thank you from the bottom of my heart.

Always, your student Ruben.

Long time *Together*

My beloved Father, it has been a long time since I have written about you.

For my heart is still empty without you. I miss your smile and your beautiful face.

Mother is with you now and my heart is still shattered into many pieces.

And my thoughts of you two being in the hands of the Lord brings some relief to my lonely heart.

You were the Father and I the son and will always try to be the son of your dreams.

Tone of Voice

What can a father tell his daughter, whom he loves more than life itself that would make her heed the words and not feel offended by them?

In what kind of language can he tell her without bringing tears of sadness to her eyes and heartbreak to her inner soul, that she is doing wrong and to slow down a little before another heartbreak comes her way again.

In what kind of tone of voice can he use that will get through and still keep peace and Love between them, in what kind, just tell me.

Hear a poor father's plea that sees and the heart- break that is tearing him apart inside.

<u>Tractor Driver</u>

What if I was to tell you that when I started school I did not know how to talk very good English? Or what if I told you that school was not preparing me for work after High School. You would probably say, yeah right, but that's what happened to me.

I learned how to read and to know the meanings of words by looking at old movies on the television. I also learned a lot of the words that I was trying to learn in school. I also learned how to listen very carefully to people because I was deeply embarrassed that I did not understand what they were telling me at all, especially when they used big words or words that I did not understand.

Please do not misunderstand me. School is a wonderful and precious thing to have, but at that stage of my life, it was not doing the job for me.

I learned the many things that I know how to do by working at them very hard.

Like in the beginning when I started working in the fields and the foreman asked me if I knew how to drive a tractor, and of course I said yes.

So he said, "Okay, start it up and take it to the other field."

"Okay," I answered him. But when he left I got on it and started pushing buttons and switches that I thought would start it up, but no luck.

Then I saw a button that I had not tried yet and when I pushed it down the tractor was in gear and half throttle so it jump up like a horse out of the gate. The only thing that kept me from falling off was the steering wheel, which I grabbed and held tight until I turned it off. By this time I had jumped all over the tomato field, which was not a good thing to do, especially if you were trying to impress your boss.

After all that jumping around I got to make it to the field, then the fun really started. The boss told the other worker to hook up the trailer and take it to the other field, but the problem was that I did not have a clue about what he was talking about. So between the both off us we hooked up the trailer; there, that was not so bad. But on the way something went wrong because somehow I lost the trailer and the pipe on the trailer. Not only that, but the man that helped me. Somehow the pin came off the trailer's hook- up and the trailer took off by itself over the rows of tomatoes in the next field. Thank God that I was not going too fast. The look on the other man's face was very scary because I thought that he was going to Kill me. Instead, we both broke out laughing. Then he said, "You never have driven a tractor before, ha!"

All I said was, "How can you tell?

1/21/9   © By Ruben Dozal Jr.

<u>Village in The Stars</u>

About thirty-eight years ago I had a chance to visit my mother's and grandmother's village for the first time. And God all mighty it was worse than what my mother kept telling me for years.

First of all, there were no roads to get to the village. We had to follow a riverbed to find our way to the village. And after we followed the riverbed for a while we reached the river and my uncle had to fire his rifle so that the barge could come across to get us. When the bargeman saw us he waved his hand and released the rope. And my uncle told us to pull the rope, which in turn was bringing the barge across the river. Then we had to pull the barge back again, which was a little harder because of the weight.

The first night that I spent there I was so excited that I did not want to go to sleep. That all changed in a minute when I went to look for my room to sleep in. Then the fun started, because my uncle brought me a cot with a gunnysack over it, which was my bed, then he showed me my room outside under the stars. I told him I needed to use the restroom. He pointed to a little room out in the back and gave me a candle so that I could see in the dark.

Then I asked where the water was because I wanted to drink some, then some more laughter. One of my cousins showed me where it was. It was a big clay vase with a cup hanging down its side.

In the morning I told my uncle that I wanted to take a shower. Then he said, "Okay, let your cousin show you what to do." "Okay," I answered. Then my cousin came out with two big cans which looked like ten gallon instead of five gallons but were only five gallon cans with wires and ropes coming down the sides so that you could pick them up. Then he brought out a big stick that would go across your back so that you could pick both of them up at the same time.

My cousin picked them up and ran to the river and I ran right behind him and when we got to the river he showed me how to use them. First, you fill one, he said, and you pick it up and then you turn and fill the other. Okay, okay, I said. So he gave me the cans on the stick. I had both of them on my back and did what he told me, but one thing he forgot to tell me that was how heavy they were. When I filled one of the cans up and tried to pull it out of the water, I did not make it and fell in the river, clothes and all.

It was a good thing that I knew how to swim because the water was pretty swift.

My cousin then asked me, "Do you still want to take a shower?" I could not answer because I was still shaking with fear that I got out okay, and besides I was a little cold.

When we got back to the house the rest of the family was waiting for us outside. When they saw me, and the way I was walking on my toes and wet from head to toe, the laughter started that lasted the rest of the day.

My cousin got yelled at pretty bad by my uncle, so I thought, until they both started laughing. That night I fell asleep pretty early from exhaustion and I did not care if my room was outside under the stars.

Around one o'clock in the morning the rhythm of drums started making noises and the people started also making noises with sticks and water buckets.

I woke up all scared and ran to my mother, asking her what was going on. She told me to look up to the moon and see how it was covered up; it was an eclipse. The natives had a strong believe in the moon eclipse. I do not know much about it except that it was a bad Omen and by making noises, it did not last very long.

© by Ruben Dozal Jr. 3/17/99

<u>Waiting for me</u>

You gave us life; we gave you headaches.
You gave us love; we gave you maybes.
You gave us warmth and tenderness; we gave you afar and distance call.
But to me, you taught me how to stand fast and fight ...fight for the unity of my family! Which at times was very shaky not to say the least in deep trouble.

Now, our father in heaven has opened up his arms and relieved you from your pain and suffering, of which you have had for a long, long time.

May your spirit touch the hands of your two grandchildren and your two daughters who are straightening their hands out to help you and take you over to meet your Nito once again.

YES, Your Nito that you loved so deeply and missed so much. You are finely together again! Please don't frown down at us for we tried the best we could to make your time as pleasant as possible, my dear and beloved mother.

My God in heaven to you and your son Jesus Christ – thank you – for giving me just a little more time to spend and receive the love and compassion that my mother & father gave me. I know they will be waiting for me when my time has come.

Thank you my God.

© by Ruben Dozal Jr 1998

We Are Not A Rock

Help! Help Me! How much can a man endure?
How much more pain can we take? We are made from the same flesh and bone like all men. We are not stone. We feel just like anybody does.

Are we so hard and solid that we cannot cry?
Can we not hold a baby without hurting him?
Can we not feel sadness when it comes our way?

We are the rock that sometimes has to hold the family together no matter what. But who holds the rock when it starts to fall?

Who can he talk to? Who will comfort him?
Who will tell him, Here come let me hold you if only for a minute?
Who will tell him, Cry my poor man, just let it all out and stand by his side, who?

Who will change his way of thinking so that he will not feel so depressed?
Who will show him that the laughter of children is good for the soul?
Who will take the time, Who?

© By Ruben Dozal Jr. 7/14/98

Where Is My Nana?

"Grandpa, is Nana sleeping?"
"Yes, mija."
"Grandpa, is Nana in heaven?"

"Yes, mija." "I answered."
"Grandpa, is Nana trying to wake up?"
"No, mija. "Because Nana was very tired and needed to rest."
"Oh." "Grandpa, is nana with God?
"Yes, mija. But we have to be good so that we can see her again."

"O.K. Grandpa, I will be good."
These little words coming from my four-year-old granddaughter, brought back all the tears that I tried to hide but could not hold back anymore, no matter what I tried to do.
"Grandpa, why are you crying?"
"Because, mija, I miss your Nana."
"Me too grandpa. Me too."

© 1/10/99 by Ruben Dozal Jr.

Who Is This?

"Hello, hello, who is it? Stop playing games, who is it?" the daughter tries to find out. But no one answered and after a few minutes the phone rings again. And the same thing happened. Two more times and the same thing over again, and finally an answer comes through.

"Hi, who is this?"

The man starts to talk real slow.

"Are you Linda?"

"No," she answered, "that's my mother." "I am Peggy," she tells him.

"Oh, yes," he says, "then you should be about seventeen years old by now, right?"

Then she really gets scared, followed by a little silence. Again the soft voice begs her not to hang up the phone. Instead he asked her "if her father was home.

She answered, "No," that her father had died in an accident a long time ago.

He then asked her, "Did you have fun at the lake last summer?"

"Yes I, I, I, how did you know about the lake?" No answer.

But another question, "Did you have fun at the Winter Ball at school?"

"Yes, I, I, hey, who is this. As she puts the phone closer to her ear she could hear the man crying, then silence, never to hear a word again.

© By Ruben Dozal Jr. 1/25/99

Why I Write This Way

I write this way because I know not another.
I make no excuses except my spelling is terrible.
I make no excuses for my sentences
that are run on together
for I don't know where or how to stop.
I am not proud of my education for
I spent some time in school.
I tried very hard to study but it was in vain.
The reason I write hard and painful is
because that's the way life has been to me.
Hard and without mercy.
I never could say to my girlfriend,
"meet me at the show" or
"here let me buy you a ice cream" or
"let me take you out to a dance,"
because I never had money to do it with.
That's what made me work in the fields and
I started being with older people.
- I miss my younger years -
That's why I became a working young man.
Working for my school clothes and gym clothes.
Working in the fields, the ever-lasting
fields of lettuce and beets.
Eight hours a day for eight dollars a day.
I worked in the fields for two years
until they asked me how old I was.
I told them fourteen, fourteen, yes I said.
The foreman almost had a heart attack.
Needless to say that was the end of work
without a school permit.
but, then I got a job
cleaning ditches for irrigation.
Ninety-five cents an hour,
twelve hours a day at temperatures of
125°, 110° or 115° ALL DAY.
With your arms moving, back bending.
But at the end of the week, PAYDAY!
The money went to my house first,
always to my house first.
This is what ended my education.
Work, always work since
I was about eight years old.
If you were to tell me this is the way you write
I would say to you fine, show me.

But, then I will tell you I write from my heart,
not from books, but what I feel at the moment.
If someone reads my words and
it moves them and they tell me so.
Then my writings have served their purpose.
But no man has ever been given credit
by his own family.
But like I said before,
I am not proud of my education and
I make no excuses.

©By Ruben Dozal Jr.   7/21/98

Why Mother?

Mother, why do you look so sad as if the light of day has left you?

Mother, why are you telling us to take it easy and not to waste food?

Mother, why is saving of money so important now?

Mother, do you not love us anymore?

Mother, why are you crying so much at night?

My beloved children, come to me and listen. Your father is going away for a while and I do not know how we are going to get along without him.

That is why I have been telling you all these things.

He is going to jail again, ha, mother?

© Ruben Dozal Jr. 6/3/99

Wife

Like in the Days of Yesterday
When our hair was black and Shiny and
Our Children Enjoyed their Infancy of Life,

But your Love for Them Was Pure and Clean and
Now That They Are Enjoying their Life in Mist of Growing up with Love In
Their Hearts,
*   And Now Our Hair Is Not so Black and Our Skin Is not so soft*
But My Love Is Greater Then Before
For I Am Still In Love With You
My Lovely Wife.

Labor Bus

I need some shoes. I need some underwear, I would tell my mother.

Oh, do not worry my son. If you get up early Saturday morning you can get the labor bus, so you better get to bed early.

All I would say was, O. K. MOM.

To me it was nothing to get up and go to work in the fields, because that's what I thought all Mexicans did. To see all the people in the morning hours trying to get in line, in front of the bus just for the chance to find a seat was a sight to see.

People coming from as far as twenty to thirty miles away just to see if they could work for just that one day, and it was heart- breaking to see them get turned down.

The ones that would get chosen would work eight hours for eight dollars a day.

Some of the sad looks of my people were in some ways the look of little hope saying, why should we continue on?

In time I would know without mistake the true meaning of the look of the faces of the ones that did not get to work that day.
The worried look about their loved ones who were left behind, not knowing if they made it back home or not.

Worrying if they would have enough to eat, and to know if they are in good health was one thing that was always on their minds.

But not one complaint about themselves, only the same question over and over again, do you know where I can get a better job?

Working in the fields at a young age taught me how to listen to my people talk about their families and the struggles they went through to get that elusive dollar for their families which all of them depended on.

And here I am worrying about my gym clothes. Somehow, this did not seem right to me.

© By Ruben Dozal Jr. 11/7 98

Let Me In

Here I am trying to understand why or why not to continue on my quest to learn more, because I am at the door. But it is not opening for me.

People tell me go seek knowledge so your work can be done better. I tell them fine, but first show me how to open the door that is between me and the door of knowledge. Please open it so that I can come in and learn how to write better.

© By Ruben Dozal Jr. 1998

Liar

Do you not hear the voices of your conscience telling you that you are lying? But, oh, I have forgotten you never lie, that's just the way people talk about you.

No, it is not true, but I hate to tell you this because you are my dear friend, but you do lie so much that you cannot tell anymore what is real and what is not.

Now you are living a lie, really hurting people bad along the way. You have to stop or someone is going to stop you cold with your lies and without mercy.

You are a master in turning things around and manipulating the truth to please yourself.

I do not.

You need help.

© Ruben Dozal Jr. 7 /12/99

Light Of The Moon

The light in the sky so beautiful and bright is just a mere reflection of what is in your beautiful eyes.

The light of the moon young love look upon feels warm, and that is what is burning within me just to have you by my side.

The cool breeze that embraces our bodies and the warm hand that touches me make my body explode with the thought that you might still love me.

Happy Mothers Day.

Your husband.

By Ruben Dozal Jr.   5/8/99

Little Kisses

We came to see and hold the other parts of our lives, one part that is separated by land and state.

We came to hold the seed of love taking everything we can for the short time that we are going to be here. Giving and receiving without distance the smiles and hugs of little bodies, hands, and kisses so wet and juicy, from little lips of love.

To my daughter and her husband, thank you, for the opening off the doors of warmth and love to us, we will take it to our hearts forever, we thank you again.

Your Family The Dozals.

© Ruben Dozal Jr   12/28/2000

Little One

Reach out and grab my hand little one.
I cannot reach it.
Wait then, do not move.
Hurry up, it is getting cold.
Okay, but do not move, okay?
Okay.
My God in heaven no rope, no knife to cut a limb off the tree.
Hurry up grandpa, I am cold!
Hold on little one, grandpa is almost there.
What to use that will hold the weight, what?
Grandpa, where are you?
Here I am.
Help me grandpa, help me!
He is going out of his mind. So he takes off his pants and belt and ties them to a tree nearby just long enough to reach down and bring his granddaughter to the safety of his arms.

Cold and shivering, just with his underwear on, they made it back to camp.

When the rest of the campers looked at him with no clothes on, it was hard to explain what had happened.

Not for the other part of his life, who told them what happened.

My grandpa, my grandpa saved my life yes, he did!

It was hard to believe this story. So they went to talk to the grandpa but he was nowhere to be found. So they called the mother to ask if her grandfather had saved her daughter from falling down the mountain and had saved her life.

The mother answered, it is impossible for my father has been gone for ten years now.

But we saw him!

Yes, we did.

©By

Ruben Dozal Jr. 7/27/99

<u>Lost Father</u>

After many years of traveling all over the country, I found myself back in my old hometown again. Why? I do not know why. Because I had promised myself that I would never come back here again.

As I walked in the dark through the street of memory I came to a burning fire in a drum and people standing around it trying to keep warm from the very cold night.

When I turned around to see some of the people standing by the fire I noticed a young man with his hands straight out over the fire trying to keep warm. A man asked him, how is your mother today?

She is fine thank you.

Are you still in school?

Yes, Sir, I am.

You are a good boy and your mother is a good mother.

Thank you, Sir.

And he walked away to be with his mother.

Poor boy, the man said. He goes to school and works so hard after school. And after all that he still takes care of his mother whom he loves so much. What else can he do for there is no other one in his heart.

The next night I arrived before the boy got there and the people who knew him were saying the same thing as the night before. But I could not say a word, just listen to their stories about him and how he has taken care of his mother.

Night after night I could not wait for the darkness hoping that the boy would show up, which he did. And always with his big smile, so beautiful that it could light up the night and respect for the people around him.

But this night it was different for he looked sad. Then one of the men asked him, was your mother sick today?

Yes, she was, sir.

What can we do to help her?

You can tell me who is my father so that I might know that he is indeed my father.

With those words he put his head down and walked away with tears in his eyes, and in the hearts of his friends also with tears in their eyes. For they were hurting just as deeply as he was.

The next night the boy is a little more himself for his smile has returned back to him. But nobody said anything, they just let it be.

Later one of his friends asked in a soft voice, do you know the name of your father?

The boy answered, yes I do.

Oh, and why do you want to know him?

Because all I ever wanted to know is why he left never to return.

And to tell him that I love him very much even though I do not know him at all. My mother always has said that he loved her and me very much, and no matter what he has done he is still my father.

But my boy, it has been many years passed and yet you have not met your father. How can you love him if you do not know him?

Because he has been in my heart for a long time now, but please do not ask me why. I can feel him close to me.

 Like I said before, no matter what he has done in his life he is still my father.
 Boy, what is your father's name?
 His name is…
 Hurry! Hurry! Your mother is very sick.
 Call for help, please call, the boy cried out which was heard all through the neighborhood.

 But the calmness of rest was in his mother's face when he got there.
 She just turned and said, thank you my son. But when she saw me all she said was, look at your son.
 Then she faded into eternal sleep.

© by Ruben Dozal Jr. 8/5/99

Love Plea

 I wish that with a movement of my hand I could make you come to me.

 I wish that with just a look I could make you follow me without questioning my reasons.

 For all these things to happen, first we have to meet. But I am afraid of your beauty, and the thought of not being looked at in the same way just tears me apart.

 I will follow the road of my empty heartbreak and all my sorrow to my lonely home and pray for the courage to talk to you, my Lady.

 The words that I am feeling in my heart might just erupt in the beauty of speech.

 I hope that the words I want to tell you fall into place for at this moment my tongue and brain are not working together. What I am trying to say is, please listen to me and my plea for love.

© By Ruben Dozal Jr.   4/19/99

Love and a Hug

You people are the soul of
caring. For people in need
of help: some that can not
take care of themselves...
some that can not see...
some that can not eat...
some that can not move without help.

The profession that you
have chosen is very unique
and hard. For all of you like in
some cases, family. To the elderly,
love and compassion are your credits.
Love and a hug is your reward.

I hope and pray that your hearts
stay in the spirit of helping people.
I also Thank you from the
bottom of my heart for the care of my mother.

You have given me one more smile
from her face and one more glimpse
of her shining eyes which make my inner
soul light up.

Thank you,

Ruben Dozal Jr.   7/28/98

<u>Missing You</u>

You taught me how to work with my hands and for that I am Grateful.
You also taught me how to stand on my own two feet, for that I owe you
my Life.

You taught respect with an iron hand and without regret, for I know now
the meaning of the word with my own children.

You were always on the minds of your children and in their hearts—for
we all Loved you in our own way.

But all this will not bring you back, sweet loving Father of mine. I just
miss you so much, my arms ache and my heart cries, just to hold you in

my arms for a second. But I will have to wait until I see you again my beloved Father.

Your son,
Ruben Dozal Jr. 8/25/98

Moon Love

Go to the river and meet me there for this is the time for romance.

The moon is in its brightest face. The scent of the Wildflowers is giving out their fragrances that mingle with the fragrance of your body, which I inhale when you come into my arms.

Come and share your love with me. And the moon will be the only witness of our true Love.

© By Ruben Dozal Jr.   5/19/99

More Time

Thank you my Dear Heavenly Father for hearing the prayer from an unworthy soul.

You have opened up my heart again, softened my temper, and made me think before my tongue gets me into trouble.

You have given me more time to spend with my Mother. This could not have happened if it was not for your Merciful Hand.

Hear me my God in Heaven, hear my humble plea and put your hand out once again, and restore my Mother back to health again.

You are the torch that leads my soul to the light, the food that I try to partake. Please do not forsake me; and give me just a little more time.

Your unworthy servant, we ask this in the name of thy Holy Son.

Amen.

© By Ruben Dozal Jr.   11/12/98

Move Like A Tree

My dear friend, what has this woman given you? It looks like you are in a daze. For a while now you have been existing, not living.

You are inhaling but not breathing the air of life, which keeps you going and thinking clearly.

My friend, we are supposed to take all the pain and sorrow that is given to us day by day and listen to the troubles of our loved ones, but that is all.

Just listen. Take it in your heart and mind no matter what pain it brings you, just take it like a sponge. But the sponge like our hearts gets heavy and cannot hold any more.

That is when we get in trouble by saying and doing things that we cannot take back. But we think that when we are saying what we have to say, we had to let it be known that what we said was right. That's when we get into trouble, my dear friend.

If I try to make things better I say to myself, you better be careful. But at this stage of anger the answer always comes back no! I was right.

© RUBEN DOZAL JR. 07/1/98

My Garden

Why don't you go outside and do something.
Like what mother? Show me.

Okay, cut these weeds out and I will help you plant a garden.

A garden. Okay, that sounds like fun. So I went outside and cleaned out the backyard, but it was hard work because the weeds were too tall and tough to cut down.

But finally it was done. The ground was ready and tilled real soft, so I went to ask my mother what to do next.

She turned and smiled and said, well, let's go out and see. Okay, now let's go and get the hoe and make some rows in the ground like this.

How many rows do I make, mom?

As many as you can, she answered. And I will go and buy some seeds, okay?

So when she got back we planted beans, corn, zucchini, and tomatoes. And with the help of some fertilizer it turned out to be a very good looking garden indeed.

After a few months everything looked nice and big and beautiful.

Then the buds started to appear and that made me very excited to finally see the vegetables starting to grow and grow. So after school I would go out and see that everything was all okay and watered if it needed water.

To my surprise, some of the vegetables were cut off and I ran to ask my mother if she had cut them off. She said no. I ran back pretty upset and started looking around for any signs or tracks that would lead me to the thieves, but I did not see anything at all.

In the following days my garden was being robbed big time. My corn gone, tomatoes, and zucchini squash all gone, and my green beans also, poof, gone. I was determined to find the thieves. So Friday night I stood watch and then it happened. I did not have to wait long to catch the thieves. But I could not believe my eyes looking at two little bodies with two bags helping themselves to my beautiful vegetable garden, just picking vegetables like in the store.

I did not say a word. And after they were done, I just followed them to see where they lived. To my surprise there were six more kids and their mother living in an old abandoned house with nothing but my food to eat for so many.

I did not say anything again for I truly felt sad and wondered what I was going to do next. The thought that came over me was too overwhelming.

So when I got home I went to the kitchen, got a bag, raided what we had and put it out the next day by the garden. The next day it was gone and so were some of my vegetables.

My garden seemed to produce more than before, but I never told my mother about the food that I was taking for the poor people. And my little visitors came the rest of the summer. One morning I went to my garden and found a little bag with a note that read "thank you" with four packs of seed in it.

© By Ruben Dozal Jr. 4/29/99

My Children's Freedom

I will not be a burden to you anymore, for my time has come.

Your wish of freedom is around the corner, so clean up your eyes and lighten up your hearts and you will enjoy the coming of a new day. This time freedom will ring in your ears.

Freedom also carries a heavy price. Indeed, you will find it out on your own by living it day by day with your own decisions.

Go now. Prepare yourselves for the joy, and the storm of freedom will be heard when you open up your eyes again.

© Ruben Dozal Jr. 6/12/99

My Man

My Man, why do you not see the harm that you are doing to your Loved ones?

Our children crying at night because of you, their Father is not home to comfort them.

And they ask how long this time Mom, how long?

My Man, the candle in my heart is still on fire for you, but you keep on putting it out. Please do not feel so sad for I still love you, My Man.

I will try very hard. And with the help of God keep the candle burning until I have you in my arms again, My Man.

© By Ruben Dozal Jr. 5/24/99

My Day

My day starts at about 4 a.m. in the morning everyday and after I get ready for work it is about 4:30 a.m. I get to work at 4:50 a.m. and make coffee for my fellow workers. Then I go in my office and start to write about whatever comes into my mind for an hour, until 6 a.m. That's when I start to work but most of the time my stories are done. If not, then I finish them at break or at lunchtime. But most of the time they are done before I go home.

At home I type them on my computer if you call my typing, typing, because it takes me about an average of two and one- half hours just to type one simple story. Then I take it to the Reading Program for corrections with my tutor Page. By the way she is fantastic.

After the corrections I go back home and do the same on my computer. After all the corrections are done and I am happy with it, the next step is the hardest and longest: to find a graphic that fits the story the best. Sometimes it takes me hours just to find the right graphic, but I do it.

Then and only then will it go into my book.

©

By Ruben Dozal Jr. 5/23/99

<u>Never Listen</u>

Come, put your head on my shoulder.

Why, is there something wrong?

No.

Why can you never do what I ask without saying is there something wrong? Just relax for a minute or two.

You never listen to me anymore. Well, you never did anyway, but just listen for a minute, okay?

I went to see the doctor today about feeling tired all the time for a while now. He took some tests and I will get the results next week.

There you go again playing with my brain and making me worry. You shouldn't have told me until you had all the results back.

But in the morning the silence of eternal sleep had come in during the night.

And she never learned how to listen.

Not The Same

It is starting to be real clear to me that the reading of poems and poetry is a dying publishing art.

People do not want to waste their time in publishing work that is not going to bring them money, _Always money._

And the work remains in the folder. People read it, people like it, but so far that's as far as it's gone with no publishing in sight.

Maybe in the years to come, maybe not.

Maybe in my life, maybe not. But until then, I will try to keep my spirit up and perhaps one day it will come through.

But I doubt very much if I will get to see it in my lifetime.

I never had any money, but I would not refuse it. I think that with it I might stand a chance of getting published. But it would not be the same as having someone ask me if they could publish my work.

Old Man

"Here, old, man, let me help you."
"Oh, thank you young man, thank you."
"Do you have anybody to take you home?"
"I do not for my children think that I am in the way and a burden to them."

"Why do you say those words old man?"
"Because I used to rule my house with an iron hand never thinking that some day I might get old and that I might need someone to help me."

"I taught them how to stand fast in their beliefs. And I forced them to finish school. I pushed them to the limit of their power to be successful in life. Always pushing, always right, never giving an inch their way. And young man, here I am old and without knowing the whereabouts of my children for I have driven them out of my life for many years now."

"Come, old man, let me take you home."
"You would do that for me young man?"
"Yes, old man, yes, for I know now what my father's words mean now, and for that I thank you. Come, let's go for it looks like rain. "
"Okay, let's go."

"You have to tell me how to get to your house, okay?"
But when the old man told the young man how to get to his house, he fell asleep.

When the car stopped the old man woke up slowly, and when he saw that he was someplace else he really got scared.

The young man went around to his side and very slowly and with loving care told him, "come, grandfather, for the family is waiting for you."

The tears from both of them just started to pour out. "Yes Grandfather." The old man did not know who he was or which one of his children were his parents.

So the old man just looked at him with glassy eyes as they both walked in the door. And the young man felt good because it had taken him five years to have finally found his Grandfather.

© by Ruben Dozal Jr.   1/31/99

On Your Own

Congratulations, you have made it despite all the obstacles you have faced head on and never given up. You have come a long way and are finally on your own. Fear not for you have learned how to fly on your own.

Now the true meaning of love will show its different faces. Hold on tight with all your strength for some of the winds can be treacherous. Please do not let the winds take you in their direction without the hope of reaching for help. Because all you have to do is straighten out your hand and someone will help you.

You are not out to show anyone but yourself that you can make it on your own, so just take it day by day like the good Lord intended it to be and enjoy it.

© By Ruben Dozal Jr. 4/2/99

<u>Only Regret</u>

You must feel some kind of relief or feel better now that your mother is gone. I mean, you have to feel free?

One Sunday after my wife made some rice, beans, and some meat I took some to my parent house. The first person I saw was my father so I told him what I had in the plate and he said good, it smells good too. Put it on the table and I will warm it up tomorrow.

Okay, dad, I answered. And before I left I asked him where was mom?

Oh, she is taking a nap.

Okay, dad, see you tomorrow.

Okay, bye.

That was the last time I saw my father alive.

And for the next thirteen years I took care of my mother who was a diabetic. I would check her sugar and give her an insulin shot if she needed one. I would also check her blood pressure and give her medication accordingly. It turned out to be a task of all tasks because then she developed heart problems along with difficulty hearing and eyesight. The final problem was having her on dialysis.

I would work all-day and then after work hurry to pick her up and take her to Salinas for dialysis three times a week.

After three hours of dialysis it would take anywhere from fifteen minutes to one hour to stabilize her, then bring her home. So my day was a very long day in all because it was another eight hours before I would get home.

Sometimes it would take some time before they could put her on the machine, especially if someone would get sick. The only thing to do was wait and wait until the other person was okay.

To watch all those poor people getting dialysis was a sight to see all the humanity suffering together. What a heartbreak to not be able to do anything.

It looked like an army hospital with all the wounded all over the place, and I do mean wounded.

My mother was a sick person for most of her adult life and very tired of it all. Everytime that I would take her to the hospital the first thing she would tell me was, "*no artificial life support,*" my son.

I spent a lot of time in emergency rooms throughout the years and never regretted one minute of it.

The only regret that I have was that I did not make it in time to see my mother go. She passed away as I walked into the room.

© By Ruben Dozal Jr. 7/16/99

PEACE

I hope and pray that when you read this letter that peace and tranquility are all over the land. Yes, even on the other side of the great oceans. This would have made me very happy indeed to have seen.

Because in my time life in some places had no meaning at all. People were being killed like cattle in a slaughterhouse, just because of different religions, or color of skin, and in some cases even because they were from a different country. This my children has been going on for five thousand years. But I hope that things might be better in your time.

My children, when you read the book in the case that I left for you, please write your part in it and pass it on to the next generation.

Do not harden your hearts to your loved ones for it will only split the family up. Let love and understanding be your strengths and your beliefs, and morals your food that will never leave you hungry.

The winds of the four directions have made it possible for you to have made it to this year, and it is up to you to reach for the stars and see if you can touch the face of God himself.

You have made it this far already and be grateful for the past generations that made it possible for you to see what they only dreamed of seeing.

One day you might think I am seeing and feeling with their eyes, feeling with their bodies the pains of the day with my open arms.

So go forth now, being content that you have read a little of your past which was as stable as a bottle of nitroglycerin. Nevertheless, we made it without destroying ourselves.

Go now, gather your family together and bend your knees in prayer

giving thanks to God for making it possible for you to see another day.
   Your Great Great-Grandfather, Ruben Dozal Jr.

© By Ruben Dozal Jr.   4/8/99

Remember The Dove

I took her into my heart when she was like a wounded dove, confused
and lost and not wanting anything from anybody.

No love
No warm hello
No, not even a kind word, but still I took a chance in loving her.

I gave her tenderness and taught her how to love because to me she was
like a wounded dove afraid of giving love. I awoke the dove with love
and caring. I also taught her how to fight for herself. Slowly the dove
turned into the almighty eagle, not caring who or what person she hurt.
 She betrayed my love.
She cheated on me with other loves, but still I kept blinding myself to the
truth of what was going on because I was addicted to loving her.

I will walk away leaving her with the burning desire to have her just one
more time. But that's all, just desire.

I hope she finds the happiness in her life that I could not give her.
That the eagle never falls, that she flies high and mighty, but remembers
once in awhile the little dove.

© Ruben Dozal Jr. 7/21/98

Madresita Mia

   Ama, why are you crying so much?
   She said, because my heart has been broken since your sister's death.
Now I stand-alone. I am old and sick. I cannot hear you, I cannot see you
very well, I cannot walk without help. I am just a burden to you and your
family I just want to die. I answered her, AY!
    Madresita Mia you have been the strongest example in my life of
strength and love. She said, Yes, but I had eight of you. Where are they
now?
   I was only one for so many years. I took care of all of you with no prob-

89

lem, but now I need someone to take care of me.

No one calls me, no one comes to see me, oh my son, I just want to die.

I just knelt down and hugged her. I told her, Oh, Mother, don't say anything. Just relax or you are going to get sick again. Hay Madesita Mia, you have to be strong and stop thinking like that because you still have me and I have you." Yes I know, but, but. No buts, just relax.

Later that night I kept hearing noise in her room so I got up and stood by the door. She was prayingd an I could hear her saying, My God in heaven why didn't you take me, not my daughter! I pray to you my God. How much more must I suffer? I pray to you to keep my children in good health and for you to relieve some of the sorrow in my heart and make the last days of my life, as you will.

Then silence, I looked over and she had fallen asleep while praying. I covered her and said,

"Good Night Madresita De Mi Alma."

© by Ruben Dozal Jr. 1998

Make Me Rich

Go ahead, jump. What are you waiting for? Just jump ha! But before you do tell me where the money is that you have and the insurance papers so that I can collect. You see I put a higher price on your life. So go ahead and jump, please. And make me rich.

Well, have a good trip.
Where are you going?

I have to go down and get ready to clean up the mess you are going to make when you hit, don't I?
Yes, but don't you care about me?

In your mind I think not, because look at you and what you are trying to do. But do not stop. Go ahead. Fifteen years of being together does not mean anything to you.

All the hardships we have faced together, what about them? Did you forget already? That's okay, jump. That way I can buy my new car. Hurry up it's getting late, just get it over with.

Hold my hand. Do not say anything you fool. Just hold me.

© Ruben Dozal Jr.   4/20/99

Stopped

Why does everything happen to me all at once, so it seems.

About three months ago I was pulled over by a highway patrol officer on a city street.

For what I wondered. But it did not take long for me to find out what was wrong.

Oh, the humiliation that I was going through! People looking at me as they drove by, and then to top it all off my pick-up did not have tags since 1997. I found them all on the sun visor.

Yes, the officer said, but they are not on your truck.

Then I could not find my insurance papers and driver's license. I was really having a bad time with all this. One thing leads to another and I was getting angrier and angrier. The officer kept writing and writing, and my blood pressure kept rising and rising.

To top everything off with a gold seal and more humiliation, when I got into my pick-up with my three granddaughters then they started on me.
Grandpa, is the policeman going to take you to jail?
No mijas.
Grandpa, when he takes you to jail can we come and see you?
I answered, No.
Grandpa, is the policeman going to take the pick-up away?
No mija.
Grandpa, are you going to cry when the policeman comes and takes you to jail?
No mija.
Okay, let's go home now.
Okay, grandpa.
No sooner had I parked my pick-up then I heard, grandma, grandma, grandpa got a ticket and the cops were going to take him to jail!

Can we go see him?

Grandma, grandpa was not wearing his seat belt and he still did not put it on. Grandma, and neither did we.

Grandma, again will you take us to see grandpa in jail?

© *By Ruben Dozal Jr. 5/21/99*

Material Things

Man, you really have it made. Look at you, a new car, a good job, no one tells you what to do, you come and go at your own pace.

Let me tell you something, young man. It only took me thirty years to get here.

The most I could ever pay for a car was no more than three hundred dollars and that was it, no more.

I was working about one hundred hours a week and that was just about right because I was used to working about one hundred and twenty hours a week, and I did it for three years. After that I slowed down to only working fourteen hours a day and I did that for twenty-four years.

Now tell me young man, how many hours do you work?

Eight hours.

You have a lot to be grateful for because men like me made it easy for laws to be passed so that you do not have to work so many long hours and can still make good money.

All you see are material things that to me do not mean not very much at all, because tomorrow I could lose it all and I still would not feel bad. And that's the way I feel young man.

To me a helping hand means more than a new car, and a smile from a person sometimes stays for years within you. And a word or two that makes an impact on your life stays forever.

Now, young man, I <u>am</u> rich, not in material things but in the memories that brought me here and making what I learned in life work for me.

So, you see, I do have it made…because I am Me.

The Stars

My mother used to tell me that when she would visit Tesila, the village where her mother was brought up in Mexico, she would always learn something new and exciting, like one clear night in particular. She would tell me they had the fire going outside and the older Natives of the village would look up to the heavens and start to read the stars and say what kind of year they were going to have. And my mother would look up too but could not see anything but stars.

Then she would ask grandma how could they see all this and she could not see nothing?

Grandma would just say to be quiet and listen.

This would make her very mad because the Natives who were talking did not know how to read or write in any language. And it would make her even angrier because they were speaking in their own dialect.

My mother told me that one night the Natives were reading the stars and all of a sudden they got up and started putting things away because it was going to rain on a clear night. She told her mother that they were crazy. Her mother just said, what are you waiting for, put everything away. Mother, I answered her, how can it rain on a clear night? Grandma just told her to do what she was told to do and to not forget to take the clothes off the line.

Son, I was so mad because it was about midnight and no clouds in the sky when all of a sudden I heard thunder and looked up to the sky but still no clouds. But about twenty minutes later it started to rain and it rained for three days.

My mother said that for a long time she would wonder how the Natives knew that because they did not have any electricity or radios, no roads to town, and no communications to the outside world at all.

© By Ruben Dozal Jr. 31/99

Beautiful Face

As you are about to leave us

Heavy with child and the beautiful glow

In your happy mother to be face

Just think: your roots will continue.

© Ruben Dozal Jr 6/12/98

Opening of my Eyes

Time has been a good teacher to me working in different jobs in the fields. Once I worked side by side with a man who was a teacher in Mexico, and it put a big sadness within me that still has an impact when I remember what he told me.

I came to see the dreams of my people, their ways of life in their new country and to see with my own eyes and experience their work with my own hands. To feel what they felt at the end of the day. And let me tell you, life is hard here in America.

I asked him, "What of the dreams that you have, if you were a teacher in

Mexico then you should be a teacher here." "Yes, I know, but I am only going to be here a short time," and with that he kept on picking tomatoes.

But the way he told me I could tell that his heart was saddened. The face of this man looking at his people and the dreams that came with them are slowly starting to fade away.

© Ruben Dozal Jr. 11/7/98

Ordering Parts

Let the light of the day put a smile on your face and speed on your fingers and patience in your tone of voice after you have all of this. OH.......I forgot, and calmness. Let the games begin, but the first rule is to keep your sanity.
Maria call extension 200........
Ruben call extension 200.......
Whoever answers call extension 200.......

"Did you order the bulk load?"

"NO! I thought you did."

"But, but O.K. Did you call this customer back?"

(face hair up at end, eyes rolling back, lips moving not saying anything)

"Oh, put these papers in the right file."

(turning around, lips still going, not saying anything)

"O.K." And here I come to make the day complete. "Can I order parts?"
"NO! NO! I SAID NO!"

© Ruben Dozal Jr   6/15/98

Phone Call

I have traveled near and I have traveled far.

I have seen some of the wonders of different people who at first sight are a lot different once you start to talk to them.

Some with happy stories and some with sad stories that just pour out of the soul like water out of a well. And some who just have to say something of no importance, only small talk.

I stopped one night at a truck stop in Indio, Ca. on my way to the bay area. When I was fueling my truck, out of nowhere two men came up to me asking if I would give them a ride to L. A. But as I turned around to talk to them, it was a sight of heartbreaking sadness.

They told me that they had been walking for three days trying to get to L.A.

Why? I asked.

Because we have a sister there who will help us, but we do not have papers. We have been walking through the desert mostly at night because of the border patrol. Can you give us a ride?

All I could tell them was that I was sorry but I could not. And when I saw their watery, sad eyes looking at me, I told them why: because on the way to L.A. there is a highway patrol inspection station for all trucks and all trucks must stop.

Then I asked them if they had a phone number to call.
They said yes, but no money to call with.

So I asked them to let me see it. Then I went to the phone, called their sister in L.A., and when she answered, I just handed the phone to them.

The transformation on their faces was unbelievable just to have heard the voice of their loving sister, who said that she was coming to pick them up.

When they finished talking to her they gave me the phone and she asked me where they were and how to get there. I gave her directions and she just said, thank you, I am leaving right now to pick them up.

I gave them food that I had bought and some money to help them out a little, and then I had to leave.

I do not know what happened to them, but when I go past that truck stop the memory is replayed again.

Poor Side Of Town

Welcome to the poor side of town, where life is a time of survival every second.

Welcome to the dreams of people, those who make it to the top. Always to the top, having money and everything that money can buy. But when morning comes and they open their eyes with cold tears running down their cheeks seeing the misery and facing reality, they realize that it was just a dream. But life goes on the same as the day before, trying to forget the dream of the night before in the poor side of town.

Welcome to the poor side of town where some of us lose all respect for ourselves and other people lose respect for us just because we live here.

Welcome, and see the children playing in the street and listen to the constant yelling and screaming, the loud noises and music in the street.

Welcome, now that you have been here for awhile and your eyes are focused and clear.

Do you not see as in all walks of life everywhere that there is a poor side of town?

The poor side of town is everywhere no matter if you are rich or poor, black or white.

The dreams of people making it are the same in the poor side of town.

Push The Button

You girls had better be quiet or I am going to stop the car and beat you up!

"Okay," Grandpa, "we are going to be quiet." But that lasted about three minutes and they started up again.

So when they were busy making noise, I pushed the button to open the sunroof and then I told them, "You see up there, the way it is open?"

"Yes," Grandpa.

"Well, I am going to push the other button and you girls are going to fly out through that hole."

"No, Grandpa, no! Grandpa, we are going to be quiet, yes we are, Grandpa."

"Okay." Then not a sound was heard from them the rest of the way home.

Unfortunately, two weeks later I picked them up from school and again the same thing happened. I did the same thing, but this time the two girls in the back seat were holding hands tight and with the other hand on the door handle also holding on tight. And the little one turned grabbed the door handle tight with both hands and said, "Go ahead Grandpa, go ahead Grandpa, push the button, yes, Grandpa push the button!"

I tried the best I could not to laugh, but I just laughed to myself. What else could I do? So I just told them to quiet down.

© By Ruben Dozal Jr. 2/18/99

True

It is true that love exists.

It is true that a smile can heal a sad heart.

It is true that a helping hand and a soft voice can bring enlightenment to a fallen soul.

It is true that saying I am sorry is sometimes harder then life itself.

Yes it is hard to say I need you, or do not go, forgive me my love, or let me love you, just give me one more chance.

Yes it is true, but giving love and receiving love is harder.

© by Ruben Dozal Jr. 3/5/99

What Can I Say?

What can I say that will soften
your heart more towards me?

What is their more to dream for
if my dreams and prayers have

been answered.

Now is up to me to keep my
dreams and prayers alive by
Loving you more my beautiful Wife.
© By Ruben Dozal Jr. 2/12/99

Yes I Am

Are you happy with me?
Yes, I am my wife. Why do you ask?
Oh, it was just a thought.
Come, listen to me my dear wife:

I married you because I loved you.

Each day, I see your beautiful face at first light. The day goes by so quickly that
I cannot wait until I see you again.
To see your smile as I come through the door makes me feel special, that you love
me.

You are my wife, and I am your husband.

Though we may not communicate, my heart is always with you.
There will be no other man in this world that will love you more then I. Always
remember that I shall always be faithful to you the way you are faithful to me.

Lies and deceit cannot be hidden from love. So to, when one person loves and the
other does not, love will not survive.
We LOVE each other!

We were joined together by the grace of the almighty and we shall stay together
as long as we strive to keep our love alive.

You are and shall always be my loving wife.

© Ruben Dozal Jr. 8/22/98

You Fool

I can see it in your eyes, in your moves, in your voice.
"What is wrong, what did I do this time?"

Do not be afraid to tell me, come out with it, tell me now?

But before you start let me tell you something.

I loved you with all my heart.

I cared for you the best I could.

I gave you what I could. I feel good when I come home from work just to see your face.

All this I have done for you and all I have been asking is that you love me for fifteen years now.

Why are you crying now? Say something!

You fool, I have been trying to tell you that you are going to be a father!

© By Ruben Dozal Jr.   2/5/99

Young Love

Do you remember the first time we kissed?
Do you remember you told me you loved me so?
Yes, my dear, do you remember the good times we had together my love?
Do you remember that rainy day we spent cuddling together at the park?
Do you remember those days?
Where have they gone? And the promises you made to me, are they gone too?
Remember my love you told me that love in your heart could withstand anything, even the disagreement of our parents over seeing each other because we are so young.
After all, fifteen is not so young. Who are they to tell us we are too young?
What is felt in the heart, no matter how old you are, no one knows the power of true love! Who are they to judge us? So come hold my hand. Let's go and tell them what you just told me, my love. No, I am afraid of losing you. Do not cry, I will tell them tomorrow.

by Ruben Dozal Jr. 5/23/98

Your Move

Wife, look at your husband now.
The one who has given you much and has asked you for nothing but love.

You never cared for him, because you are lost in your own world.
You never know where he is.

You are never at his side when he needs you.
Now is your chance to get out, now that his life is hanging by a spider's web.

Now that he is all broken up and cut up beyond belief this is your chance Wife to cut out and go.

Take it now or stay and try to be a wife and a
Woman to him or, just go.

© *by Ruben Dozal Jr.   7/11/ 98*

Still The One

I am the one who came.

I am the one who was looking for help.

I am the one who left pride outside.

I am the one who did not know why, why, for I do not no the driving force that is pushing me on.

Yes, I am the one who stands out above all in the family as the strongest and meanest.

Yes, I am the one who has fought tooth and nail all my life to better myself.

Yes, I am the same one who without asking would lay down my life for my loved ones in a minute.

But hey, I am still the one. I cannot change myself but I can improve on myself for tomorrow, so help me my Almighty God.

© By Ruben Dozal Jr.9/14/99

Talking To The Wind

With the bitter taste in their hands I, I saw them deteriorate into the walking dead, so it looked like because I saw them.

I saw them fade away into nothing, seeing things that were not there.
And I would find them talking and fighting in the shadow of the wind at
all times of the day.

I saw them get beaten up by people who were offended by their words.

I saw them lying in the dirt, in streets and in cars which they could not
get out of because they could not find the door handles to open them and
get out.

Yes, I saw them. All and one was a year younger than I.
I know, for I helped carry his coffin.

Yes, the bitter taste was great and so are the memories that come to mind
when I go past the cemetery and remember how they got there. Good old
bitter taste,

The Winner Again.

© By Ruben Dozal Jr.   9/17/99

The Other Man

After working all day in the fields on Saturday and getting paid the
same day, it felt good because I now had a little money to go to the dance.
But that thought quickly changed when I would get home and was
asked by my father, *where have you been all day?* Working, I would answer
him.
Why didn't you tell me, my father would ask me.
I could not answer for I knew that tone of voice all too well, because
he had been drinking again.
Drinking would change him into this man who was foul talking, not
listening too me or my mother, always saying that he was the man in
charge.
Then I asked, didn't you give me permission to go to the dance?
Are you crazy or what! I knew then to keep quiet because I knew my
father's temper, the scars of which I carried all over my body as the

reminders of his anger.

Here I was fifteen years old and still could not go to a dance with my friends.

The tears would sometimes be tears of deep sorrow, not because he did not let me go to the dance but because the drinking would change my father into a stranger to my eyes and put a deep pain in my heart.

I Loved my father deeply and respected him strongly, but when he drank and the other man would show his ugly face, I would tell myself, I will never be the other man, so help me God.

© Ruben Dozal Jr. 9/19/99

The Stars

My mother used to tell me that when she would visit Tesila, the village where her mother was brought up in Mexico, she would always learn something new and exciting, like one clear night in particular. She would tell me they had the fire going outside and the older Natives of the village would look up to the heavens and start to read the stars and say what kind of year they were going to have. And my mother would look up too but could not see anything but stars.

Then she would ask grandma how could they see all this and she could not see nothing?

Grandma would just say to be quiet and listen.

This would make her very mad because the Natives who were talking did not know how to read or write in any language. And it would make her even more angry because they were speaking in their own dialect.

My mother told me that one night the Natives were reading the stars and all of a sudden they got up and started putting things away because it was going to rain on a clear night. She told her mother that they were crazy. Her mother just said, what are you waiting for, put everything away. Mother, I answered her, how can it rain on a clear night? Grandma just told her to do what she was told to do and to not forget to take the clothes off the line.

Son, I was so mad because it was about midnight and no clouds in the sky when all of a sudden I heard thunder and looked up to the sky but still no clouds. But about twenty minutes later it started to rain and it rained for three days.

My mother said that for a long time she would wonder how the Natives knew that because they did not have any electricity or radios, no roads to town, and no communications to the outside world at all.

© By Ruben Dozal Jr. 31/99

This Time

For the love of my drinking that became my only passion in life, I thought that it was my friend until I lost everything that I had and loved so dear to my heart.

For the dryness in my throat day in and day out kept me taking in the taste that would make it stop.

For the tears and tears of my wife and children who were afraid of me when I was drunk.

For all the trouble and sadness and heartbreak that I ran over like a twig on the road, not feeling anything but only seeing the road for my next drink ahead.

For all this that I did and the trouble that I caused I am going to stop taking in the water of destruction.

I hope to God for the strength to do it this time so that I can regain the love and respect of my loved ones again.

This time I will do it!

© Ruben Dozal Jr.   9/28/99

Three Minutes

Kiss your partner goodbye and if you have Children, kiss them too.

If they are asleep cover them and take a good look for they are the ones that you are working for.

Take the whole three minutes to see them all. Do not forget you might not get to see them Again.

So take the time.

© Ruben Dozal Jr. 3/27/99

Too Young

You are all too young to remember me and to know the way I felt when I held you in my arms.

You are too young to know how much I love you.

You are too young to understand the words of this old man who yells at you and who tells you not to do that, or this. But it is because you are so young that I try to help you.

Maybe when you are not so young you will read these words and say, my grandpa was right. We were too young to understand, but he loved us anyway.

© Ruben Dozal Jr. 9/21/99

Truck Stop

Let me tell you about one of my more delightful experiences when I was a truck driver. I was hauling lettuce at the time from Imperial County to the bay area. And it was around March toward the end of the lettuce run and my youngest brother wanted to come home with me, so I said okay.

A little way past Indio, Ca. my brother fell asleep and about an hour later I had to stop, so I pulled into a truck stop and restaurant by the highway. But this one was different: this truck stop had a Big dinosaur Rex on the parking lot and I parked right under it. Then I woke my brother up and asked if he wanted to use the restroom, and he said yes.

So I opened the door and got out and I waited until he got out. Then I just started running and yelling, screaming, telling him look, look up, and when he saw that animal right above him he took off running like greased lightning, falling down, screaming and yelling. I had to tackle him to stop him. For a while there I thought that it was not a good idea to have done this to him and I felt bad. But it was fun!

A while after he got his color back and calmed down we could not stop laughing, but it still took me a little more time to get him back in the truck. After that every time that I would stop he would look up in the air to see if there was anything up there.

© By Ruben Dozal Jr. 2/26/99

104

Let it Go

Why do you cry now?
It is too late.
Because I miss them.
Yes you do, but what happened when they were alive?
You never had the time to come and see them, always the same excuse: maybe I will go to see them.
So save your tears when they come your way. Do not forget that you have kids too and it's nice to hear their voices now and then.
Please do not tell me I know how you feel because you do not.
None of you were there when I would take her to the hospital in the middle of the night and stay there until all the tests were done, sometimes till sunrise I'd be there and then go home. And sometimes I would take her right back to the hospital after work and another day without sleep.
None of you were there to see her happy heart when she would talk about us all and the way she loved us. It would make her cry in deep sorrow for she did not feel loved in the same way.
You were not there when she would tell me please, son, let me go.
You were not there when in order to make her feel a little bit better I would make her tell me stories about her life. This would sometimes ease the pain, but this you do not know because you were not there.
The pain that some of us feel or some of us felt is going to stay with us for a long time to come, but the memories will never die.
I was the son who was there; not too well liked, not too well loved, not too well dressed, not too well mannered, but nevertheless I was there to the end.
Now let it go and stop feeling sorry for yourself.
For they are Free and walking hand in hand in the house of our Heavenly Father.
   Yes, let it go.

© Ruben Dozal Jr. 9/27/99

No Food

Newspaper mister?
No, not right now.
Can I clean your windows?
No, thanks.
Hey, mister do want me to clean your shoes?
I told you already, no! no!

Why do you keep on bothering me?

Why?

Because we are hungry, my brothers and sisters and I.

But I will not steal to feed them.

With a tear stuck in my eyes I told him, show me.

This way please mister, and to my surprise indeed there they were, the other part of his life, waiting for him to bring in the bread of the day.

When I saw this it made me feel less than an ant.

Why don't you get help?

Because they will take my brothers and sisters away and I will never see them again.

But I will not steal to feed them or myself.

I have to be around to help them and I cannot do it in jail.

This time with a tear in my eye I told him, wash my car and I will help you.

© By Ruben Dozal Jr. 8/31/99

No Problem

Boy, how do you do it?

Do what?

Well, every time I see you, you are so cheerful and happy with no problems in your mind at all, no problems.

Listen to this. My wife is having an affair with another, no problem.

My children are having children with no father to be seen, no problem. My son alone has three with no wife, no problem.

They come and go as they please. My house is in shambles, no law, no respect for my laws or me but no problem.

The only real problem is my breathing the air of life that is all, just breathing. But hey, no *problem!*

© Ruben Dozal Jr. 6/12/99

Penny Wise Drugs

With the utmost gratitude and sadness in my broken heart I am writing these few lines to you and your staff to thank you all for the wonderful kindness you gave to my mother and me during her illness.

You and your personnel were a big help in getting her medication right all the time and in telling me how to give it to her.

It is not so easy for me to write these words for my heart is still aching in pain.

I am deeply sorry that I did not do it sooner.

Please accept my apology and once again, I thank you from the bottom of my heart.

© By Ruben Dozal Jr. 8/25/ 99

My Father

He was left orphaned at the age of eight. This happened to my father.

He and his brothers and sisters were tossed from place to place because no one wanted to take care of them. Yes, it happened to my father.

His father, being a teacher, did not know what to do with them, and the only help he had was the bottle. Yes, it happened to my father.

As time went by he learned early in life to take care of himself. Yes, it happened to my father.

He worked in a shop at an early age just for room and board. Yes, this was my father.

He never gave up the dream of some day being somebody, so he worked cutting hay and alfalfa hay at night for many years. One day, the tractor that he was driving broke down and he fixed it without even thinking about it. And that was the greatest change in his life, because he got put in the shop as a mechanic. Not too much pay as a mechanic, but still a better position in life.

He would work many long hours a day to get ahead. He had to with eight children to support. Yes, this was my father.

Then one day it happened when someone reported that he was an alien and his whole world got turned upside down. Yes, it happened to my father.

So we all got sent back to Mexico, and my father found us a place to live until he could find out what to do. But he never gave up. He went to the American counsel in Mexico and asked for a passport. They gave it to him because of his work, but it took time to get it because he did not know where he was born. Yes, it happened to my father.

After he got the passport he continued to work in the U.S. for another five years, until one day he got stopped at the crossing and was asked to go the office. He thought that he had done something wrong, but it wasn't that. It was that his passport had *expired. And when they called out his name, the secretary thought they had told her to call San Francisco. How she heard that, my father said he didn't know.*

She did, and it turned out that my father was born there and had the birth certificate sent to him. Yes, it happened to my father.

But still it took my father another two years to get all the papers fixed because by this time my younger brother was born in Mexico. Yes, it was one of my father's happiest days.

But still another two years went by until my father was given the okay to move back to his country. Yes, this happened to my father.

Then one day my father lost his passport, so we had to go to the immigration office. My father, for the first time in his life, came out with tears in his eyes because not only had they found the rest of his papers, but they also told him that three more of his brothers and sisters had been born in San Francisco. Yes, it happened to my poor loving father.

Now I wish I had him to tell him how much I love him. I would take all the punishment gladly just as long as I could hold him in my arms, if only for a minute.
He was my father, with hands of stone but a heart full of love for his children. I know that now, for I am the son who feels the same way about my children and my grandchildren.

I wish, I wish.

I Used To Be One

Here, let me see that!

Are you afraid to hold the handle or what?

No, but it is hard.

Yes it is, and it will not get any easier if you do not get to work.

I suppose you can do it better than me?

Yes, I can, but I am not the one who is getting paid to do it. So get with it now because it is getting late and the weeds are still standing. Hold the shovel's handle tight and attack the weeds the way you would attack me, and you will see it won't be so hard after all. But you have to start now.

Oh, Dad this is really too hard for me. Come here, son, put the shovel in the ground. No, no, push it down. Okay dad.

Now you see that was not so hard, was it?

No, now leave it there.

Are we done?

No, not yet, but go and bring me the other shovel and I will help you clean and cut the weeds.

Yea, that sounds good to me dad.

The son runs to get the other shovel and when he gets back sees his father on his knees and asks what are you doing dad?

Just remembering, the father answers, just remembering my son.

But when the father brings his face up with tears coming down his cheeks, he looks up at his son standing there with the other shovel in his hand.

Remembering what dad?

Asked the son for he has never seen his father cry before.

Tell me dad, tell me.

I used to work with one of these shovels for many hours a day so that we could eat and live.

But dad, that's the kind of work that jiggers and wetbacks do.

Yes, my son, you are so right, now take a good look, what do you see?

Nothing dad, I see nothing.

Give me that hat. Now, my son, what do you see?

Yes, it is true I used to be one of them. And my son, this is part of your heritage. Do not be ashamed of it, but learn how to use it and be proud of who you are.

Now, my son, look at me, what do you see?

I see my father.

Yes, my son, but learn how to see the man and not what he or she looks like or what kind of race they are, but what can this person teach me or what can I learn from them.

Now my son, the weeds are waiting for us for they are our real true _Enemy._

© Ruben Dozal Jr.   7 /2/ 99

I Will Walk

Mother, why can I not move and play with other children?
Why do I have to put these things on my legs to walk?
Why do I have to use these sticks to hold me up?
How long am I going to use them Mother?
What are they for, tell me please, tell me Mother how long?
My Son, come here and sit for a minute and I will try to tell you.
With tears in her eyes and her hands on her chest the mother starts, you are a special Boy, my son. This is only a test to see if you really want to be like the other boys. And if you do you have to try harder and be stronger, so you can get stronger legs my son.
So it means I can walk and play like the other kids if I try harder.
Yes, my son.
Mother, is it going to take long for me to get strong?
No, my son, no. You just have to try and get strong at your own pace, my son.
Mother, what if I do pray. You think that God will hear me, do you mom?
Yes, my son, he will hear you.
OK mom, then I will pray for the little boy in my class that does not have anybody to help him, because he is just like me but his parents died in an accident.
Mother, are you going to leave me too? -
No, my son. With tears building up and her heart beating faster than before, the mother could not hold it any longer and just started to cry, bringing her son close to her.
Mother, the boy tells her, _I will walk._

©1998 Ruben Dozal Jr.

If I Could

If I could dream and make my dream come true I would dream for heaven and earth to be together as one. And people would treat each other as people and not like animals the way we treat each other now.

Yes, if I only could.

If I could see the future I would eliminate hate and prejudice and replace it with love into the hearts of mankind.

Yes, if I only could.

If I could fly, I would fly upwards, upwards to the heavens and touch the face of God himself.

Oh, yes I would, if I only could.

© By Ruben Dozal Jr. 8/10/99

<u>Ignorance</u>

I am one of so many of my people who has brought himself up in the presence and dealings of drugs and alcohol.

I will tell you about one incident that happened to me that still shocks me until this date.

I was a truck driver and warehouseman for a chemical company at the time.

I came in late one night to help the other warehouseman to clean up and close up, so I just started cleaning up and putting things away. On the desk was a bag of chemicals, which I picked up, and put away and then cleaned up the desk and put everything in its place. When I got back there was some more white powder on the desk again. By this time I was a little upset because I had just cleaned up the desk. So I got the trash can and put all of it in it and I thought to myself, there, clean again.

Then here comes the other warehouseman, and when he saw what I did I swear he almost died. When he asked me what happened to the powder, *I told him to look in the trashcan. So he ran over to it and said, do you know what you just did?*

Yes, I said, I cleaned up the desk and do not get it dirty again.

No, no, do you know what that was? No, I answered, and I do not care.

That was coke, he said, and I was cutting it for a friend.

And like I told you before, I do not care.

Do you have any idea of what you did?

Again with the same question.

What did I do?

Only that you threw a lot of money away, that's all.

What am I going to do now?

© *Ruben Dozal Jr.   6/14/99*

Illegal

We came to work; we went through all kinds of hardships just to get here. We take work that no one wants. We do not ask for Welfare. You can only see the pain of the body, but not the pain of the soul and spirit. Is your heart so darkened and your blood so cold and your hands too stiff to straighten them out to help a fallen man? Fear not, because it will not hurt you. We might be different races, but nevertheless we have dreams just like you. We also love just like you.

We did not come to steal the work from your people; we came to help your people with their work. All that some of us ask for is work, that is all. We do not benefit from Income Taxes and in some cases we cannot even go to the doctor. We cannot collect Disability Insurance. We do not have any benefits at all. We still work hard to feed ourselves and the American people.

We are still treated like dirt and still we do not give up. Some of us even try harder to prevail and get ahead. Some of the bosses, when they do not want to pay us all, what they do is call the Border Patrol and we are gone that quick, so easy.

The next time you sit down to eat do not forget you might be eating food maybe picked, packed, and cooked by an illegal worker.

© Ruben Dozal Jr. 11/11/98

In Your Hands

Why do you not look up to the wonders of the universe?

Look to the hillside, see the deer in peace with nature.
Look at all the things you have done. Put them all together and in reality you have seen plenty. But not enough. You still feel that there is something left undone.

Something that is not complete as you search for the answers. You close your heart and turn off your ears and put blinders on your eyes. At the end of it all, tired and beaten, the mind in a daze, the light begins to get brighter. But it is too late. You have been searching all your life for something that you have been living.

But your heart was cold, feeling nothing for love and your ears were without sound, closed and never hearing the pleas of people trying to help you. And your eyes not seeing at all the troubles you were causing and the friendships that were destroyed.
Yes, the light is getting brighter but the damage has been done. The only thing to do now that you found yourself is to live life the way your senses tell you and be happy. After all, you did find yourself.

© Ruben Dozal Jr. 7/10/98

In Name

Hey, I am your father.

Yes you are, you gave me life, but that is all you have given me.

I remember running to you when you got home from work and you would always tell me, *I am too tired to hold you or maybe later I will play with you.*

That maybe never came to be.

I remember you telling me, *go outside and play because I want some time for myself.* What about our time together, time that you never had, what about that?

Time that cannot be replaced and time that brings back sad memories of what could have been otherwise good ones.

It is funny how the time changes and now all of a sudden you have the nerve to tell me that you are my father. Where have you been? You have always been my father but my loving Father, not.

How can there be love if you never had some or showed any for us?
What I really want to do is reach inside of you and grab your heart and
just squeeze it a little so that you will feel the same way I felt, for the
many times you told me I do not have the time.

That pain, which you will feel, is the pain that is still within me.

Yes, you are my father but just in name only and I'm your Kid.

© Ruben Dozal Jr. 6/25/99

Into Darkness

Time and time alone sometimes cannot heal a broken heart. Sometimes it
cannot, for the mind has to help in the healing also.

The treachery and betrayal that robs the heart from a state of unhappiness into a state of shock can devastate the whole person into a state of
limbo.

Not caring or listening to the power of self-healing can only cause
depression, which can make a person, sink deeper and deeper into the
misery like a bottomless pit. Never to see the sunrise or sunset or a new
day, for the bitterness in the heart has covered everything into darkness.

© By Ruben Dozal Jr. 8/27/99

Just One Time

Just one time I loved in my life.

Just one time I held you so tight in my arms.
Just one time you told me that you loved me.

Yes, just one time sweet love of mine.

Just one time we kissed so softly and tenderness was the way we felt.

So please, do not let this feeling end; Let's start over again just one more
time.

Sweet love of mine.

Just The Word

I do not have any riches. I do not have a car or a house that I can call my own.

No loved one that I can call and tell how I am. No one at all.

What you see before you, this is the way I come.

These hands of mine will work hard for you. My heart will be in your hands to do as you will.

But within me will leave the everlasting love and care that I will freely give to you. My love, just say the word and let God help us do the rest.

That is all, just the word.

© Ruben Dozal Jr   1998

Laughing At Us

The big hunters, my two brothers, nephew and I were all supposed to go hunting and swimming about one mile and a half away from home, to the big canal where we knew the water would be cool and swift.

Things did not work out this way at all, because on this trip we took along my dog. He was jet black like a black bear and the size of his head was as big as a bear's. A little way from home, being the oldest I got a terribly smart idea: why not let the dog pull us on our bikes? So I tied his rope to the handlebars and we started riding and walking along the ditch bank. As we continued on our trip I had my bother on the bike with me when God knows what happened. All we saw was a rabbit.

And the ride was over.

That dog pulled my brothers and me on our bikes and my nephew who was walking in and out of the drain ditch and under the fence where we got all tangled, up in barbed wire.

Needless to say, our arms and legs were all scratched up. We looked like we had gotten into a cat and dogfight, and we were the losers. It took us about an hour to get untangled.

We were all cut up and bleeding and crying all at the same time. After we got loose we still had to try and walk back home. Knowing the temper that my mother had, I feared for my life. So we picked ourselves up and started back home. We looked like a group of refugees from the war!

When we did make it home and saw my mother coming toward us, all I said was, we are dead. But all she said was what in God's heaven happened to you kids?

So we started to tell her the story. To our surprise she did not hit us. But the medicine that she used on our cuts was worse. It was called medqurio. Like Iodine, it was red in color and used to cut infections. Let me tell you, that stuff burns and burns, and to me it was worse than getting a spanking from her now famous broom.

One cried out, no more Grandma!

The other screamed, no more mom, it's his fault. Still another cries out, please no more mom. That stuff was mean!

Monday when we went to school the school nurse took us home because she thought that we had been abused. That all changed when she talked to my mother and older sister.

Then the bad news came that we had to go to the doctor and get a tetanus shot. We all thought it was going to be a breeze.

It was, but afterwards we could not move for days because of the pain on pain. And every time we saw that dog we swore that he was laughing at us.

© By Ruben Dozal Jr. 7/31/98

His Mighty Hand

My dear and Loving brother, it was with great delight to read your letter.

Heaven and earth cannot take the love that I have for you because that's the way that Mother brought us up.

116

Whatever you have put in your heart about me, you put it there by yourself and only you can take it out.

It seems like yesterday that we walked and played in the fields of barley and wheat, and swam in the canals.

Keep your faith up and your mind clear so you can witness the miracles of God's mighty hand.

Your brother Ruben.

© By Ruben Dozal Jr. 9/12/99

Hold on Tight

Seasons come, seasons go,
people come, people go.

Friendships are made, up
friendships are broken up,
but our love will withstand
all the obstacles that come our way
hand in hand together as one.

Hold on tight my love for the ride
is about to start up again.

© Ruben Dozal Jr. 2/11/99

I Am American Born

The next part of my life, I do not like at all. This is because my eyes are open and my ears are clear.

The way that people talked to me all of a sudden became clear. It hit me like a spike right through my heart and could not stop the words.

They just kept on coming and the spike kept getting deeper and deeper until I could not take it anymore. So I started fighting back with words of my own, and my words were not of good taste to anyone, especially me.

I hated to talk like them. But when you are called "Greaser," "Wet-back, go back to Mexico," you "Dirty Mexican," my fist would get tight, my eyes would get watery, and my body would start to twitch. Why are these people telling me these words? I am American born!

117

I live here, went to school here, worked in the fields here. So I brought myself out of that kind of talk and just started fighting more and more and got to be real good at it.

Then when I started working more often my anger started to cool down, but I did not have any friends to think of.

The spike that was put in my heart is still there, and when it starts to ease out slowly bringing the cold hearts of the people that put it there, I start to feel good. But it always seems to happen that someone finds a hammer and puts it right back deeper than before.

I pray that before I die that the spike will be removed from my heart so that I can see the real love of people and their loving hearts, and better treatment for my people.

We are not all dumb Mexicans.

© Ruben Dozal Jr. 8/4/98

I Gave You Friendship

You gave me a smile.
I gave you friendship.
You gave me friendship, and
I am giving you words that
To some might mean nothing, to others
the difference between a happy or a sad heart.
We will miss you all.
You have been a joy to work with,
but no one can foresee his or her destiny.
No one can predict tomorrow.
I hope your job change brings you contentment at long last.

Your Friend Ruben

© by Ruben Dozal Jr. 4/18/98

I Have Arrived

If they only could see me now, that with hard work and blood from my hands that kept me going, never giving up. And the sweat from my body, and the aching bones of my back, and above all, the discrimination that I have been through, to have had a boss tell me to my face that I would never be nothing but a dumb Mexican.

If they could see me now, just to see that it was not so, that I was not a

118

dumb Mexican, but a thinking man with respect and giving respect back the same way.

If they could see me now that the words that were said to me gave me the strength to prove them wrong, just to say, Hey thank you, for if it was not for your downgrading me I could not have survived the next chapter in my life.

I feel that all men, no matter how they appear to be physically or in appearance, no matter what, given a chance they might change the world.
I know not where the power comes from for me to say or write these things that happened to me, for they just flow out of my mind.
If they could see me now, for I am without hate, for I have found my own tranquility and knowing without a doubt that I have arrived.
Yes, if they could see me now.

© By Ruben Dozal Jr. 1/18/99

I Have Done This

On my way home I saw a man working in the fields driving a tractor and I thought to myself, I could do that.

Later on I saw a man moving sprinkler pipe and I said to myself, I could do that.
As I continued on my way I saw a truck driver unloading some tractors for the fieldwork that needed to be done and again I told myself, I can do that.

As I looked to the right side of the road I saw the wild oats in the field and a combine cutting them down and I told myself, I did that.
When I turned to the street that lead me home I thought to myself, I have done all the things that I have seen.

Dear God, you really have blessed me and brought me back in your own way to remember my humble beginnings and to look back and remember my roots as a farm worker.

© Ruben Dozal Jr. 8/14/98

I Am Learning

You have been teaching me how to use
Proper English and for that I thank you.

Please keep being patient with me
Because I am a slow learner.

You will find that no other student
Will have more respect for you than I.

Thank you for helping me.

Your Learning Student.

Ruben Dozal Jr.

© Ruben Dozal Jr.   12/19/98

I Am Yours

The bright twinkling light of the stars in the blue heavens as they take
over the tired day brings a thought or two about our happy times together, my sweet love of mine.

And when the moon shows its beautiful yellow face, a sensation of passion awakes in my inner soul that I cannot control for I am yours and you
are mine.

And the love that burns within me has not gone dim one little bit, because
the fire is still burning in this heart of mine for you forever, my Loving
Wife.

Come and hold my hand, but be careful for I am still on fire for you.

© Ruben Dozal Jr.   10/6/99

I Hope

We came to see the new arrival of my seed, and arrive it did for it was
a boy.

120

The first male of my seed, know that he is here with the blessing of our heavenly Father and prayers from his loved ones. He can only come out ahead in life.

He has already the best of two worlds and two cultures to make him strong. It is up to the mother and father to teach him the full potential of their heritage with respect and honor, never being afraid of the truth but embracing it to it's full strength.

My grandson, I hope that your mother and father tell you about your grandparents and some of the perils of life that they have gone through.

Your Grandfather

© By Ruben Dozal Jr. 8/5/99

I Humbly Ask

Oh my God, who art in heaven, please look upon my poor soul and give me the strength to continue to see the light of day. Please do not darken my steps for they are like those of a child that needs to get back on the path.

Please give me the patience for my fellow man, because at this time I feel so lonely and forgotten. My mind is working so fast and my heart is pumping so hard that I can feel it trying to come out of my chest.

Please, dear God, all I ask is for you to help me find tranquility within me, just one more time, so that I can find peace of mind within my poor soul.

I humbly ask this in the name of thy son.

Amen.

©By Ruben Dozal Jr. 8/18/98

I Love Me

I have seen them cry.
I have seen them happy.
I have seen them jump.
I have seen them fall.

I have seen the sweat and heard their cracking bones.

I have seen them big and small.
I have seen the determination in their faces, never giving up.

I have heard them say, you are doing fine, don't quit this time, you are almost there. Just a little bit more, and more fuel is pumped into them.

I have heard them cry and cry and just give up, no matter what you say to help them.

I have heard them say, my mother loves me and so does my husband. And I love myself, so what's the point? So they get their clothes and leave.

This losing weight business, it's hard!

© Ruben Dozal Jr.   9/23/99

I Still Love You

Have you not seen the things that I have done for you?

The love that stills burns within me.
Do you not feel warm inside when I am close to you?

Or is it all gone from your heart? If so let me know so we can continue on our separate ways. Because you like me are entitled to some happiness; perhaps that's what you want. Do not prolong your decision, it will only make it harder at the end.

Do what you have to do and make it quick, because in my Heart will always be the burning feeling to hold you next to me, to feel your body next to mine.

The inner feeling that only a man in love can feel for his mate, but the pain of being rejected will burn even deeper and it will take him a long time to love again.

©1998, by RUBEN DOZAL JR.

Bits and Pieces of My Life

In the year last of the forties, I was born to Maria and Ruben Dozal, a humble couple by today's standards but headstrong in those days.

According to my birth certificate my father worked as a mechanic for the eastside garage, my mother was a housewife, and both were described as white Mexicans.

They had four daughters and four sons.
Rachel, Norma, Elizabeth, and Bertha
Rudy, Ruben, David, and Rafael.

I will try to write to the best of my old mind some of the things that happened to me during this not so clear time. Please read on.

In the early fifties I remember starting school, but then one day our world got turned upside down and it has never been the same again.

Because at that time we were being deported to Mexico which I did not understand and nor tried to. All I remember was seeing my mother crying and crying and me selling newspapers in the streets of Mexicali to try and make ends meet.

My mother kept on crying and before long, five years had come and gone. But in 1957 the crying stopped for a while because this was when my younger brother Rafael was born.

Then without warning one of my sisters died. Still, I could not understand why.

All the sadness, and for the first time I saw tears in my father's eyes. After some more time of sorrow, shame and words that I could not understand that were said to us which were humiliating, I still carry in my mind as fresh as the day I heard them for the first time.

Miren un refugiado de los Estados Unidos.

Which means, *come and see a refugee from the United States.*
Miren un Gringo Mexicano.

*Which also means, look come and see a Gringo Mexicano who does not know
how to speak English or Spanish. Miren a un Pocho. Which means, come and see
a half-breed.*
*They would make fun because in truth I did not understand them, sometimes
at all.*

Time after time I would play with no shoes on my feet and time after
time something would always happen to me. My feet carry all the scars
of disobedience, oh yes they do.

One time in particular stands out in my mind of not listening to my
mother. She said don't take your shoes off because your father is coming
home early and we are going to town, do you hear me?

Yes, mom.

No sooner than she turned her back, my shoes were off that quick
because I hated to wear them. And away I ran like the wind only to cut
the top of my toe all the way down the side of my right foot.

I did not want to say anything to my mother and father, so I hopped
across the yard to the water and tried to clean it off. But the bleeding did
not want to stop, so I made a mud ball and I put it on my foot, which
stopped the bleeding.

Little did I know that the next day my father was going to take us to
Tijuana to visit his uncle.

But his uncle was in Ensenada and lived by the beach. All my brothers
and sisters were barefooted except me, and that was unlike me, so my
mother came over to me and asked me why I wasn't out playing with the
rest of the kids I just said that I did not feel good, but when she saw me
walk with a limp she said, come here. Then she said, take your shoes off.

No, mom, no.
You cut yourself, didn't you?
Yes, mom.

Okay take your shoes off, she said. And in doing so the smell that came
out was terrible to everyone near and far.

124

Oh my God, oh my God, because of the heat of my feet being in my shoes it created an infection so bad that they thought that I was going to lose my right foot, and I started crying and crying.

By this time the cut had turned inside out and they could not use stitches to close it up.

It took three days of cleaning all the mud off that I had put on it, so in the meantime they were giving me one shot of penicillin a day for infection.

My father then said, we are going to my other uncle's home farther down the road. And when we got there I had a high fever and my father's uncle's wife told one of her boys to hurry, go to the foot of the mountain and bring me these herbs. Now hurry, hurry, go, go!

When they got back she boiled all the herbs and gave some to me to drink and then took all the wrapping off my foot and put it in the water.

In two days the infection was gone and my fever was gone also, but I still could not put my shoes on.

After we got home the next day I was taken to the doctor and he said that I almost got gangrene, whatever that meant. He said I would have had to cut your foot off. And that cured me from ever taking my shoes off, for a while.

The doctor did not stop there. He cleaned my cut again and gave me another shot of penicillin.

He also told my mother that if he had to sew me up that it was going to take about twenty stitches or maybe more.

This is only one thing that happened to me in the fifties.

On another flying accident that happened to me, oh yes, I was the invincible Superman who was climbing the tree right outside our home.

They said that I must have been about sixty feet up on that tree and that's all I remember. Because when I woke up I had straps all over my upper body because I had fallen down and broken my collarbone and almost broke my right arm. Oh yes, I looked like a mummy all wrapped up.

That's not all. Then the kids would come and say what happened Superman, did you run out of air? Or does it hurt Superman?

That was the last time I climbed a tree for a long time.

All this happened to me when we were still living in Mexico.

But when we came back to the U.S. my troubles did not miss a beat.

My father found a house on the outer limits of town and we loved it because there were four huge eucalyptus trees and irrigation canals on both sides of our house.

This is what caused my next accident. My mother had gone to town and before she left she looked at me and said, stay away from the canal did you hear me?

Yes mom.

But I must have misunderstood her because the water looked so clean and running so smooth that I just jumped in. The water felt so cool for it must have been at least one hundred degrees and getting hotter.

When I moved my arm to swim I felt a sharp pain but did not think anything about it until I came out of the water, looked down at my right arm and oh my God, I had a huge cut on it. Oh, I would say at least five inches long and deep, and again I got some dried dirt and put it on to stop the bleeding.

By this time I was so scared that I ran inside the house and got an old tee shirt, cut it up and wrapped my bleeding arm in it.

When mother got home I was taking a nap, so she thought, and I did fall asleep, not awakening until the next day.

I went to school like that and my mother never saw my cut. But when I was sitting down the teacher walked by and saw the blood on my arm, so she took me to the school nurse. Since I did not understand English very well I thought she was just going to clean the cut but instead she took me home.

When I saw my mother I just started to cry because I knew that as soon as the nurse left that I was going to get beat up and I did.

After beating me up my mother called a taxi and took me to the doctor. The doctor took one look at my cut and said, oh my God kid, what did you do? And I tried to explain. When I saw the syringe in his hand all I remember saying was, no! No! But mother's hard look made me stop quickly.

It took the doctor about an hour to clean my cut but then he gave up and told my mother, your son is very lucky because by putting the dirt on the cut he stopped the blood or else he could have bled to death.

126

Still after all that I knew that I was going to get beat up again when we got home, on that I was sure of- - and I did.

I wish that I could write everything that happened to me in the fifties, but read on because here comes the sixties.

In the sixties the awakening started to come about, not so much in education of school but in the education of words that were said to me over and over, the meaning lost to me in the ignorance of not being able to understand them.

This harsh reality made me walk alone all through my teenage years.

When I started to understand some of the words, sometimes they would make me cry and sometimes they would make me double up my fist and fight. Oh yes, I did. And more than my share. But I am neither ashamed of it nor am I proud of it. But I did learn how to fight.

In the sixties I lost a few friends who got the call to Viet Nam. My sister's boyfriend on his first tour of duty stepped into war was no more, for his life ended right on the beach.

A few months later my cousin's boyfriend's life also came to cease in a rice field where he stepped on a mine. And the sad thing about it was that it happened also on his first tour of duty.

My name also came up for the draft three times, but I think that it was not in the stars for me to go.

First because I was still in school, then because I was married and had a baby on the way. After that because one of my ears had a hole in it that I had received when I was swimming. A friend of mine jumped into the pool without knowing that he had hit me with his knee on my left ear and just blew my eardrum out. And because of that I almost drowned, but they pulled me out of the pool. I did not know what had happened but when I woke up and tried to walk I could not keep my balance. That's when they took me to the doctor. The doctor told me the reason that I could not keep my balance was because I had a hole in my ear and that's why my equilibrium was off.

After a year or so it got better but it kept me out of the service for good. Yes, it truly happened to me in the sixties.

I learned many skills in the sixties that I still use today. I moved sprinkler pipes working a hundred hours a week for five years. I drove forklifts, tractors, caterpillars, and tomato machines I also drove trucks, the big trucks, eighteen-wheelers and pulling a low bed trailer. They call it a Cozack, moving equipment all over California.

I also learned plumbing and welding that I still use today, along with fabrication, which makes my mind think a little more, and I love it.

All this I learned in order to eat and keep a roof over my family.

In the sixties I also met my wife. She was my brother's sister- in- law and I did not think too much about her until we went to a dance in 1968 on a Saturday night and the following Monday I asked for her hand in marriage. After thirty-three years we are still together. My God in heaven, what a beautiful war it has been!

I wish that I could say that everything was okay, but that would be a lie. Here we were in the eyes of God All Mighty, my wife being only fifteen and I nineteen, and I did not know if we were going to eat tomorrow or not.

Because after we were married it started to rain and rain with no end in sight. I being a farm worker and also this being the first time on my own in this area, I did not know about the rainy season. After a month of this we did not have any money for food, not even money to buy kerosene for our one burner stove.

Sometimes when we were cuddled up together because of the cold weather and no heat, my tears would just start to flow from my eyes, sometimes until morning.

Let me tell you this was one of the darkest times in my life, but this gave me the fire to improve myself and keep fighting for a better life, not ever, ever forgetting my roots as a simple farm worker.

With the rain still coming down I borrowed some money and told my wife, we have to move out of here or we are going to starve to death.

So we loaded all our things in my car and away we went, still saddened by the departure but what else could we have done?

We got to my hometown in the morning and rested the rest of the week. But I still looked for work and found a job driving a tractor at night. My hours were going to be from six pm to six am.

The night work, all alone at night, would bring about thoughts of tomorrow so deeply that at times I would shed a tear or two, because by this time my wife was heavy with child.

Then the dark clouds of tragedy came over us and have never left. The clouds of death settled over us and kept taking and taking our loved ones without mercy. First my wife's grandfather passed away, followed shortly by her grandmother. Her brother passed on, followed by her other brother, and also her other brother who was shot at a party.

After that her father got killed by a motorist who never was found.

Her uncle and aunt followed, then two cousins followed by her other aunt. Then my nephew was killed, followed by my father's death onto the hands of our Lord. Again the call was out and another one of her aunts passed on, followed by three nephews and her brother-in-law, followed by my brother-in-law. But the winds of death did not want to leave yet so their force still took my sister at the hands of her son, followed by my broken-hearted mother.

And finally the breeze came back and took my other sister, younger than me.

So I know death and the heart that is drained and filled up only to be drained deeper than before. So I do know death.

My all mighty God, what a test of pain and suffering we have gone through but we never let go of your brilliant Torch that is lighting our way in the midst of the immense sadness of our souls. How can we not see it? How can we not see it?

In the following months, and working at night, I could do almost nothing without thinking about my wife and our baby.

Sometimes when I would get home and into bed I would put my hand on my wife's belly and the baby would start to play soccer inside, moving all over the place.

Just the thought to me of having my own child was more precious than gold, because to me it meant that my seed was going to continue even at this young age. This was my choice to be a father and to be a father when I was still young. And I was going to be one soon.

By the beginning of summer my wife and I were back in her hometown in which I felt like a stranger, and thirty-three years later I still feel like a stranger living in the town of my children's birth.

In June of '1969 we were blessed with a baby girl. I named her after my grandmother, Angelita Maria and called her mis ojos, which means my eyes.

Soon after that I got a job as a row crop spray driver.

Spraying insecticides on row crops and working again at night, I hated to work at night because it was taking me away from my wife and my little girl. But what could I do, we had to eat.

So I worked and worked but when there was no work at night I would spend the day working in the shop.

This was the opening of the tree of knowledge to me because I started learning how to weld by just watching other men do it. I learned how to plumb pipe together and thread it so they would fit together.

The most important thing to me was that I learned how to listen better to people and my fellow workers.

The education of books had stopped almost two years before but the education from work never stopped. So my mind was like a sponge trying and trying to learn more skills to help myself in life.

I saw men using cutting torches, welders, and other men doing plumbing. I would see all these things being done and believe it or not, that's how I learned all the skills that I have today by saying, if they can do it so can I.

In the coming months I learned how to drive a truck and trailer, which turned my whole life in a different direction for all times.

It took me one year or a little more to get my class one driving license because of all the questions and trying to read the book. But I did pass the test and I did get my license.

My God has been at my side ever since because then I got another job with a garlic company delivering garlic products all over the bay area.

Then I started pulling a trailer taking prunes to the dryers which at times was fun and at times very scary because some of the orchards were hard to get in and out of, and more difficult when the truck was loaded. I lie to you not.

Sometimes you would make a turn and when you would look back you would see the trailer off the road or off to one side and sometimes completely off the road. Now that was one of my most scary experiences since I started driving truck and trailer!

One morning when I got to work my boss was there waiting for me with a funny look on his face, and right away I knew that I was going to be laid off. But it did not happen that way at all. Instead, he said, the driver did not show up again and I am tired of it. I want you to go with this driver so he can teach you how to drive this big rig, okay?

I did not know what to say.
Okay? He asked again.

Okay, I answered and, and, thank you.

So I went home and got some clothes and told my wife the good news. Then my wife asked, when are you coming home?

All I said was tomorrow I think. That tomorrow never came to be because I did not know that a loop meant unloading in L.A. and loading up again in the Imperial Valley, then back to L. A. and unloading again, then back to the Imperial Valley, and then and only then would you load back to the bay area.

But I learned the routine quickly and those years got to be the most unforgiving years in my life, until now. Because I knew very little about my daughter's first seven years and that has stayed in the corners of my heart, never letting go.

When my wife told me again the news of us having another blessing in our house, shortly thereafter I quit my truck driving job out of the area. And back to the fieldwork I went again.

Soon after, because of my skills, I stayed working in the shop and little by little I started driving again, but locally until it started to be too demanding.

And like before it came to be a full-time job. And ten years came and went in all that time that I drove trucks for this company and never was I late. I always made my deliveries on time and I made this company a lot of money.

When I asked for a raise, I was told that it was out of the question. But it was time for me to move on anyway and move on I did, quitting my job not knowing what the road of my destiny had in store for me.

Armed with only the skills of my hands and a strong back I went forward only looking back at the things that I had done.
Little did I know that we were in the middle of a recession and work

was not to be found that easily.

After some closed doors did not open for me, I did find one that was open and I took it and started working for another chemical company. But this one was paying me a lot more than the one before and I stayed there for two years.

But it started to put a bind on our budget because it was out of town and I had to commute one hundred and twelve miles every day to and from work.

So I started looking for a job closer to home, and just by some miracle I found one in about a week. I took it and this was the downfall of my steady work for another two years.

Because I would work and then I would not. But I could not leave it because it paid so good when I did work. That's why I stayed with it until I could no longer do it, and again I looked for another job. As a matter of fact that year I had seven different jobs and all turned out to be dead ends. In most of these jobs the companies would go under or move out of town, until I took a job as a maintenance man and this changed my life again forever.

By this time I had made up my mind that the next job that I was going to do would be maintenance or a mechanic. And it worked out for me pretty good because at the next job I was a truck driver and a maintenance mechanic.

As I worked as a maintenance man my brain just started to get educated in the area of fixing equipment and how to fabricate with more confidence.

Just as I was on top of the world the winds of fate gave me another blow and down I came for the count for the company that had given me this chance went under and once again I was left without work.

Hurt by what had happened so close to the holidays, I took whatever work there was and back to the wheel I went.

I thought that this job was going to be steady and it was for almost a year. But when I was going home one day my boss told me, we are going to move and I want you to come with us.

I said no, and gave him the keys to my truck right there and then. Again I found myself looking for a job. So in desperation I went back to my old job and just playing around I asked my old boss if there was a job for me.

And he said yes, when can you start?
All I could answer was, tomorrow.
Okay, he answered, and another year went by that quick.

By this time I had been behind the wheel for twenty-four years and was getting pretty tired of it. I could not see a way of getting off the truck so in the meantime I started looking for another job.

It took me another year to find one that might bring some changes and it did.

I was supposed to have started working for another chemical company as a truck driver, but they had not yet gotten the truck so I started doing maintenance until the truck was bought. Two years came and went and I was still doing maintenance.

In this chemical company it was a whole new adventure because it was completely different in the way they did their packaging of chemicals and preparations for customers. The most exciting thing I was part of was building a distillation column first with help, then I was left all alone to finish it not knowing anything about it much less making it work.

It was a job in itself but I did finish it and I did make it work.
Later on I improved it far above the designing and engineering blue-prints. This made me feel good.

The engineer came back later and could not figure out how I made it work. He did not tell me this but he told my boss and my boss just smiled.

The engineer asked my boss if I was an engineer also, because the way I made it work only an engineer could have figured it out. My boss did not say anything.

All I told my boss was I am done now but I need a programmer to program the P.L.C. because I do not know how.
And when the programmer got there he was looking for the engineer, so my boss told him, go see the mechanic and he will tell you what to do and how.

And I did. Then the programmer turned to me and asked me, you must have had a degree in engineering to make this thing work. Again I did not know what to say, but I did make it work and it stayed working until now.

Oh, and by the way, I did not finish high school, but it does not mean that I cannot think.

Since this date I have built two more machines and helped to make them work right.

Through all these years I have learned the hard way that you will always be looked down on because of your education. But because the good Lord kept me a step ahead of them, they never caught up with me.

The downgrading finally took its toll on me and I decided to move down the road looking for a new job. Shortly thereafter I found one, thank God, and I am more calm, less stressed and doing fine.

Four years ago I started writing about whatever came to me and those simple words are still being written with my own hand.

My spelling is still terrible and my sentences sometimes are too long, my grammar is my grammar. I forget about commas, periods and some of the funny little looking marks in writing.

I have made an effort to write the right way, but when I start to write a story the words are all laid out for me in my mind. But when I put them on paper that's when I get in trouble. Because the hand does not follow the brain very well; they each want to go their own way. But I am trying hard, believe me I am.

In 1998 when I started writing I had no idea what the out- come was going to be. But when I showed one of my stories to my granddaughters' day care teacher she asked me, who wrote this? And I said, I did. And this was the turning point of my writing adventure in life.

She told me about the Reading Program and how they help adult learners to read and spell the right way.

At first I did not want to go because of my age, which was old, but I went anyway because I wanted my stories to be spelled in the right way and with the right grammar. And this is what the challenge has been to me. While the light of day still shines on me I will try to do it.

After many years of silence and nobody I could call my friend I started this class and perhaps that is why I am still taking this class for it has really opened my mind to the wonders of words. I am not afraid to try and spell although sometimes I spell words wrong. But that's okay now because I can look them up later in the dictionary.

Words, which I had no clue as to what they meant but sounded good to my ears. And thanks to my tutors I learned the meaning of them and also how to spell them correctly.

The simple words that I write I feel down deep within me were supposed to be written and that duty fell on me. And I have no way of knowing why and this I tell you in truth.

For the words just flow from my mind and I try to translate them onto paper to the best of my ability.

At times I feel that the learning process is like a small stream of water flowing down the mountain, small and independent. But slowly it is given a push by another stream and the speed starts to pick up a little, winding in the mountains, hitting rocks and other obstacles in its way, but not stopping.

The stream finally reaches its destiny, perhaps to a calm and serene lake or the thundering sounds of the majestic sea.

My journey is the stream in the mountains slowly but surely reaching its destiny.

With a push here and a push there and a tear here and a tear there that I would shed when an obstacle was overcome, I could feel the burden in my heart ease off a little.

They tell me that I have come a long way in my writing, but I feel that I have not yet written the beginning of what I am supposed to write.

The thoughts are many and the words of choice are even more immense.

In the confines of my solitude when the mind is at ease, the thunder and lightning start to rumble. And without thinking about it a tear in my eyes appears just thinking of all the things that have happened to me and I am still here.

And I try to write these things down to the best of my ability. Since the day I took my woman to be my wife and bear my children the ever-lasting struggle to better myself has not stopped only gotten stronger.

From not having food to feed my wife and only five cents in my pocket, and on top of all this a child on the way, my heart has not given up.

I have the most powerful corner that will not let me down no matter how hard I get hit or dragged on the ground because I will get up, I will clean myself up and get ready for the next blow.

And I know that my corner will not turn its face on me if I do not turn my face on it, but embrace it as another round.

My Lord, your mighty hand has brought me a long way in clearing the road of confusing words and putting them down for me to pick up and to put them down in my own way, so that all who read them can understand them without a doubt.

Dear Lord, you are He, whom we look up to and ask for help, but we forget to look to the sides because there You are also.

You have opened my simple mind and have given fire to my hand to write so that all may understand my words.

This I will do until you close my eyes. But I will not fear the darkness because I have tried to live in the light all my life.

The windows of knowledge have been cleared with the tears of my heart and the boiling anger of my blood, because every time I tried to get ahead there was always something in my way.

But now it does not matter because my heart has been rekindled to face the obstacles in front of me. So calmly I think of a resolution and keep going with a smile on my face instead of boiling over like a volcano.

The winds of the four directions have given me the ever-lasting thoughts of life and have delivered them to my head and burned forever in my mind.

I do not know the outcome of all this. I do not know what is going to happen with all my words that I had time to put down on paper for all to read. I do not know.

The truth is that my hand is still on fire and I cannot turn it off.

© Ruben Dozal Jr 12/6/2001